QA1.M8325

0 0068 00056774 0
Mathematics and the rea
Whitworth College Library

S0-CAE-828

ISR 68

Interdisciplinary Systems Research
Interdisziplinäre Systemforschung

DISCARD

Bernhelm Booss
Mogens Niss
(Editors)

Mathematics and the Real World

Proceedings of an International Workshop
Roskilde University Centre (Denmark), 1978

1979 Birkhäuser Verlag · Basel, Boston, Stuttgart

CIP-Kurztitelaufnahme der Deutschen Bibliothek

Mathematics and the real world: proceedings of
an internat. workshop / Roskilde Univ. Centre
(Denmark), 1978. Bernhelm Booss; Mogens Niss
(ed.). — Basel, Boston, Stuttgart: Birkhäuser,
1979.
   (Interdisciplinary systems research; 68)
   ISBN 3-7643-1079-0
NE: Booss, Bernhelm [Hrsg.]; Roskilde
Universitetscenter

All rights reserved.
No parts of this publication may be reproduced, stored in a
retrieval system, or transmitted, in any form or by any
means, electronic, mechanical, photocopying, recording or
otherwise, without the prior permission of the copyright
owner.

© Birkhäuser Verlag Basel, 1979
ISBN 3-7643-1079-0
Printed in Switzerland

Introduction

In earlier times perhaps only philosophers or philosophically inclined people used to raise questions about the interaction between "mathematics" and "the real world", about the interrelation between concept and experience, between theory and action, about the meaning and truth of abstractions and of constructive thoughts. Only recently has the "real world" turned these theoretical problems into practical questions about the character and the prospects of mathematical activity.

The mathematical community is presently under considerable pressure. Our students are questioning whether our work is meaningful; some of our fellow mathematicians are dissatisfied with their own activity, with the arbitrariness and lack of objectivity in publication and career criteria; colleagues in other departments demand readymade mathematical techniques; and, from outside universities, a practical utility of our teaching and research is being urged. On the one hand, we find those who regard mathematics as a miracle remedy, and on the other hand those who would totally reject mathematical methods in favour of computer outprints, statistical recipes or general common sense.

Within the mathematical community, the reaction to these problems is rather diversified: Some mathematical circles recognize in the demands from outside only "the anti-intellectualism of an inane world", against which "the outer order and beauty of mathematics" has to be defended like a dream of flowers. Others are willing to adapt immediately to all demands, from whatever quarter they may come, in order to get the desired funds or positions, maybe even by promising the impossible.

It was the aim of the Roskilde Workshop to bring together a limited number of people having attitudes somewhere between these two extremes, people

– who do not shut their eyes to the fact that the development of mathematics is now worldwide and that mathematics has become applicable on a large scale, thus constituting an integral part of the cultural and scientific infrastructure of any country and becoming one important part of the technological basis for agriculture, industry etc.,

– who are conscious of and concerned about the problems with mathematics in itself and with its relations to the world at large – problems generated by this greater involvement of mathematics,

– but who share also a relatively optimistic attitude towards the possibility of finding a productive answer to many of the questions raised.

The Workshop was organized at Roskilde, close in space and time to the International Congress of Mathematicians, held in August 1978 in Helsinki, and was sponsored by the Danish Mathematical Society, the National Research Council, the Danish Ministry of Education, the Rectorate of Roskilde University Centre, and the Institute of Studies in Mathematics and Physics and their Functions in Education , Research and Applications of Roskilde University Centre, IMFUFA, which undertook the organisation. The Workshop provided a platform for participants, (mostly) mathematicians, from many countries and from many different fields to exchange views, experiences and good ideas. This being a very untraditional meeting, treating very broad questions in only two days, neither very definite conclusions nor concrete decisions concerning further coordinated activity were to be expected. Most problems were of such complexity as to allow only rather divergent discussions, based on differences in views and concerns of the participants.

The documents of the Workshop thus reflect to some extent the present methodological situation, i.e. our still very limited knowledge *about* mathematics. Nevertheless, they should serve as an encouragement for continuing discussions elsewhere and as a basis for further work along the lines suggested at the conference.

The editors wish to thank research librarian at Roskilde University Library Else Høyrup for having elaborated the bibliography included in this volume as a follow-up to an exhibition of books *about* mathematics which she kindly prepared for the Workshop.

We should also like to thank Ian Cocker for his help in checking the English manuscripts for this volume.

The editors.

Table of Contents

Acknowledgements

In addition to participants and persons involved in organizing the workshop, the following persons have given useful advice and encouragement in the preparation of the workshop. We wish to thank these persons for their help.

Egbert Brieskorn, Bonn. Head of the Department for Mathematics at Bonn University.

Eric Burhop, F.R.S., London-Geneva. President of the World Federation of Scientific Workers, CERN.

Ta Quang Buu, Hanoi. Professor for Mathematics and Former Minister for Higher Education.

John Coleman, Kingston (Canada). Head of the Department for Mathematics and Statistics at Queen's University and Former Chairman of the Exchange Commission of the International Mathematical Union (IMU).

Lothar Collatz, Hamburg. Former Director of the Computing Center, Mathematical Institute and Institute for Applied Mathematics of Hamburg University, Member of the Deutsche Akademie der Naturforscher (Leopoldina).

Gnadi M. Dobrow, Kiev. Visiting Professor at the International Institute for Applied Systems Analysis, Vienna-Laxenburg.

Albrecht Fölsing, Hamburg. Director of the Division for Science and Technology in the Federal Television Service (NDR-Wissenschaftsmagazin).

Horst-Eckart Gross, Bielefeld. Secretary of the Project "Berufspraxis des Mathematikers — Mathematik in der Industriegesellschaft".

Erhard Hampe, Weimar. Head of the Department for Civil Engineering at Weimar School of Architecture and Civil Engineering. Chairman of the Committee for "Tubes and Tanks" of the International Association of Shell Structures (IASS).

Leif Johansen, Oslo. Head of the Institute of Economics at the University of Oslo, Member of the Council of the Econometric Society.

Jean-Pierre Kahane, Paris. President of the University of Paris-Sud (Orsay) and Coordinator for Europe of the Exchange Commission of the International Mathematical Union (IMU).

Klaus Krickeberg, Paris. Department of Mathematics, Formal Logic and Informatics at the University Rene Descartes (Sorbonne). President of the Bernoulli Society for Mathematical Statistics and Probability.

Harold A. Linstone, Portland. Future Research Institute of Portland State University. Senior Editor of the Journal "Technological Forcasting and Social Change".

Horst Matzke, Weimar. Chairman of the 8th International Congress on the Applications of Mathematics in Engineering.

Michael Otte, Bielefeld. Head of the Institute for Educational Studies in Mathematics of Bielefeld University.

Boyan I. Penkov, Sofia. Secretary General of the Bulgarian National Committee for Mathematics.

Prosper Schroeder, Luxenburg. Director of Schroeder & Cie. Consulting.

Lynn D. Spraggs, Montreal. Simulation Research Group in the Department of Civil Engineering at Mc.Gill University.

Nicolae-Victor Teodorescu, Bucharest. President of the Union of Balkan Mathematicians and Chairman of the Science Policy Committee of the World Federation of Scientific Workers.

Erol Varoglu, Vancouver. Faculty of Applied Science of the University of British Columbia.

Trevor T. West, Dublin. Head of the Department for Mathematics at Trinity College. University Representation in the Upper House of the Irish Parliament.

Hans Zassenhaus, Columbus. Director of the Computing Center of Ohio State University.

Bernhard P. Zeigler, Rehovot. The Weizmann Institute of Science, Department of Applied Mathematics.

O. Structure of the Workshop

The Workshop was arranged in four sessions chaired by the editors of this volume. Each session was opened by panelist contributions, which for the first three sessions are printed below.

The following questionnaire was presented to the participants in advance in order to structure the debate.

Bernhelm Booss, Mogens Niss

Catalogue of Questions

1. Session: The genesis of new mathematical concepts, methods, and techniques in the course of our century.

What have been the conditions for the emergence, development and spreading of new mathematical knowledge?

a) Perhaps more new mathematical results and whole new mathematical disciplines have been emerging during the last 50 years than in the previous thousand years of the history of mathematics. Many of them — such as information theory or optimal control — have emerged from outside traditional mathematical institutions. Some new disciplines have had immediate success while, for others acceptance has been slower. Some developed on the grounds of more or less well formulated older problems, some were generated in order to tackle new problems coming from the urgent needs in practical life. What sort of general statements could one make on the development of mathematics in retrospect?

b) In his Paris talk of 1900, David Hilbert affirmed the unity of mathematics, "this always self-repeating and changing play between thinking and experience". How effective has this "interplay" been in the course of our century? What have been the effects of the capacity of mathematics to provide itself with problems – and what have been the effects of the impact of practical questions on mathematics? How to evaluate the scientific, budgetary and moral aspects of the struggle (and convergence?) between the theoretical and the pragmatical attitude?

c) "My experience has been that theories are often more structured and more interesting when they are based on real problems." Probably most mathematicians will agree with this opinion expressed by Donald E. Knuth, because mathematical activity without emotional perspectives becomes boring, as does every other unmotivated human activity. But there still remains the question, to be answered best perhaps by looking at the history of mathematics in this century: What is it that makes a problem "real"? How can the practical relevance of theoretical results be evaluated? How well has the inner mathematical crediting system functioned? What have been the main criteria in judging the quality of the results of mathematicians in the eyes of their fellow mathematicians? And what has been the set of criteria for mathematical work in other sciences and in the practical context?

d) What have been the attitudes that have brought about decisive progress in the field of mathematics and in mathematics application? Are there distinguishing marks of the "exemplary mathematician" (such as "clearness of conception", "allinclusive view of phenomena", "creative imagination", and "perseverance")? Or has history shown a rather broad spectrum of attitudes, a variety of very different mathematicians' personalities?

e) What has been the relation between the capacity to find appropriate inner mathematical abstractions (mathematical axiomatization, conjecturing, proving) and the capacity to find the right extramathematical or premathematical abstractions (modelling)?

f) The common lament on the "growing specialisation" and the "information avalanche" in mathematics needs careful examination: What has been the connection (and the contrast) between specialisation on the one side and deeper penetration in one problem on the other side? How decisive has been the breaking down of earlier specialized points of view and the taking of new views? And is the orientation over some fields of mathematics or over mathematics as a whole today easier or more difficult than in the beginning of our century? The same question applies to the environment of mathematics: How far are the consequences of a mathematical result surveyable?

2. Session: The future of mathematics.

What kind of hypotheses and ideas can one venture regarding possible ways to solve present contradictions in the process of mathematical creativity?

a) Which of the major trends in mathematical activity discussed in session 1 seem to be rather stable, and able to supply a basis for extrapolation of the future development of mathematics and its relations with the non-mathematical world? Given the continued increasing mathematization tendencies both in other sciences and in practical work, where the efficient use of mathematical tools is sometimes becoming decisive for the acceleration of progress for the particular field, one might ask: Which contradictions are about to be sharpened by the growing practical expectations and demands — and which may turn out to be overcome more easily under the pressure of urgent prac - tical needs?

b) How reliable will be the following "extrapolation": (i) The branching process between "pure" and "applied" mathematics will continue. (ii) Pure mathematics will develop rapidly and broadly and asymptotically independant of practical needs and experience. (iii) The development of applied mathematics will be rather slow and depend substantially on the further progress in pure mathematics. (iv) Manpower applied to the solution of practical problems with the help of new mathematical methods and manpower applied to "data retrieval systems" continuing with some sort of systematization of mathematization and of mathematical knowledge might be more difficult to compensate for by computer "intelligence" than some sort of pure mathematical research?

c) Nowadays two approaches in the application of mathematics seem to be very sharply distinguished. Firstly one can try to deduce the most far reaching conclusions from most minimal assumptions or, secondly, one can start with a very practical problem, generalizing the question step by step, paving over the problem area with a variety of mathematical theories by hand until the problem becomes transparent and workable. Is there a possible spectrum between these two approaches? And what institutional conditions could lead to more flexible approaches?

d) It might be impossible to gain a total survey over the state of mathematics. But does there exist a theoretical system to deduce systematically some general structure covering all mathematical theories or disciplines thus leading at least to a macroscopic survey of all present mathematical fields? What are the prospects of "transformation theories" mapping one area of mathematics structurally on to another, enabling a comparison of results and deficiencies of one area with results and gaps of another? Does there exist a procedure to structuralize the still unsolved mathematical problems, starting with a catalogue of unsolved problems with or without "significance" evaluation? Is it possible and manageable to make an overall correlation between the corpus of mathematical results and leading concepts in the "mathematization" on the one side and observed or expected properties and relations within the real world, the physical, biological or social "matter" on the other side? Could such correlation serve as a guide in "prospecting" useful new mathematical models or concepts? And can one venture a tentative prognosis, which mathematical domains will expand most rapidly in the forseeable future?

e) If something has to be changed, what is more urgent: other mathematical theories and results — or other types (or another blending of types) of mathematicians?

f) What is the impact of the different social systems on the development of mathematics?

3. **Session**: The proliferation and popularization of mathematical results within the mathematical community and toward "users" of mathematics.

How to develop a strategy for a more appropriate "allocation" of mathematical knowledge to people lacking it? How to transfer mathematical results into other disciplines more rapidly — and how to use practical experience gained from one field more systematically for applications in other fields and for inspiration in mathematical research?

a) In some major areas of other sciences and of practical work, is a determination of the most necessary or desirable mathematical knowledge in principle possible? How to distinguish between the most advertised and the most essential points?

b) How to conduct — as with industrial products — a marketing or scientific social analysis for "mathematics", i.e. a systematical analysis of the needs of "appliers", of their capacity and performance difficulties and of the conditions to be fulfilled for covering the demands?

c) "In general the mathematical results that have the widest impact are not technically the most difficult." This statement of Michael Atiyah leads to the question of how to distinguish in a concrete field between the "very line points which present great technical challenges to the specialist" and those aspects which are "of interest to the general mathematician" or those providing the necessary elements of a working knowledge towards applications?

d) Economic conditions and traditions of publication have brought up a kind of polarisation within the production of mathematical literature: There is generally a strong predominance of elementary books as well as of prestigeous research reports, whereas the medium range of advanced comprehensible and intelligible introductions in modern areas seem to be largely under-represented. Furthermore, all authors with ambitions in the middle range are not equally succesful. How to collect and propagate good experiences in publishing? What's necessary that good examples no longer stand isolated? How to transform the "art" of good publishing into a "science", into a systematical branch of human productivity?

e) How to procure higher prestige for the working up and popularization of mathematical concepts, methods and techniques?

4. Session: Discussion and initiation of concrete initiatives.

What can be done in continuation of the work done in sessions 1 - 3?

a) How to gather a list of people who are excellent mathematicians, and who understand a wide range of applications, and who work in a corresponding way as academical teachers? How to collect their experiences, their lecture notes etc, — as a basis for application-oriented, theoretical education?

b) How to work out a catalogue of those mathematical disciplines and know-ledge most urgently needed in developing countries?

c) Could one make some proposals to the leading bodies of the International Mathematical Union, the International Federation for Information Processing, the Bernoulli Society for Probability and Mathematical Statistics etc., initiat-ing some series of joint colloquia or other coordinated or parallel activities?

d) What possibilities are there for the production and distribution of a small, cheap international debating forum communicating on a very elementary level those new ideas and methods which are discussed within the mathematical community and which might have interest for a more general scientific or culturally interested public?

1. Factors Inside and Outside Mathematics which are Important in the Generation and Development of New Mathematical Disciplines

Leopold Schmetterer

The Development of Mathematics and its Social Economical Background

In the discussion I want to introduce explicitly a new element which does not seem to be included in the interesting catalogue of questions prepared for the first Session. That is the social economical background. I think that even in mathematics this background is of greatest importance, not only for the early development of mathematics but also for the tremendous achievements and new mathematical ideas in our century. I claim that basically the emergence of a new field in mathematics always follows the same pattern. When the economical development of a human society has reached a certain level, problems of an empirical origin occur. The human mind is then able to develop methods belonging to a branch of applied mathematics by means of which these problems can be mastered. When this branch has reached a certain maturity, then mathematics as a discipline in its own right emerges from here. The beginning of this transition is due to outstanding personalities. When mathematics itself has reached a high level, this transition from applied mathematics to a new mathematical field may occur on a very high level of abstraction. Moreover the empirical background of this field may sometimes be rediscovered only by tracing back a long chain of development. When science in human society has become an important tool in handling a large number of very diversified problems, tracing back the empirical origin of a mathematical discipline may for instance be possible only by considering intermediaries like physics, biology, social sciences and so on. Finally I would like to point out that the axiomatization of a field in mathematics on a high level of abstraction does not mean that this mathematical discipline has reached a point of "no return". Axiomatization of a mathematical discipline is certainly not possible without a profound understanding of its logical structure and the relationship between its concepts. Its achievement, however, further leads to innermathematical applications and new mathematical discoveries. Moreover, the experience at least of the last century has shown that even the most abstract ideas "remember gratefully" their remote origin and finally allow important applications in fields outside of mathematics.

I think that a careful study of the relation between the cultural and economical situation on the one side and the development of mathematics on the other side would yield interesting results and add a new dimension to the history of mathematics.

I am going to illustrate some of the general statements by means of some well known examples and some very sketchy considerations.

As far as we know the development of arithmetic and geometry in ancient Egypt and Babylon was entirely determined by the needs of an early agricultural society and a quite impressive military machinery. All these simple mathematical considerations are of an applied nature but this material was the base of the Greek mathematics from which mathematics as an independent science finally emerged. I think it is not accidental that this development took place in the Greek cities. It is very well known that Athens at the time of Pericles was a big trade center with a flourishing industry. Gifted people had the possibility to think about abstract mathematics. The great Greek mathematicians finally arrived at the most advanced form of abstraction by establishing axioms for mathematical structures. The Elements of Euclid were still taught during the Middle Ages. Since 1500, new concepts in geometry, but also in other fields of mathematics, have been developed, due mainly to a fast

increasing interest in corresponding practical applications. This interest is related to the rise of the bourgeoisie and to the transition from the medieval
feudalistic society which was based on agriculture to a society whose economy was determined by small manufactural work. As far as mathematics is
concerned, this development reached its climax with the great mathematicians of the 17th and 18th century. I restrict myself to mentioning only
Newton, Leibniz, the Bernoulli's, Euler and d'Alembert. In a certain sense
these great mathematical geniuses were all applied mathematicians or mathematical physicists — at least from the point of view of modern abstract mathematics. I think that this is even true of Leibniz who also paid attention to
axiomatic ideas. But these giants in mathematics opened the door to the development of modern analysis as a mathematical branch in its own right. Let
us still make the well known observation that Newton's concept of the Flu-
xion is closely related to the Indivisibilia which have already been used for
centuries by practicians. With the consolidation of the industrialized society
in Europe at the beginning of the 19th century the interest in abstract mathematics rose again and finally led to a phenomenal development of mathematics.

The modern probability theory and mathematical statistics provide a good
example of a branch of mathematics whose origin can be found in problems
of non-mathematical fields. Simple problems in game-theory were the guide to
Laplace's probability definition which was based on the concept of equidistri-
bution. An industrialized society needs statistical data concerning population,
fecundity, social status and so on. It fits very well the framework of the lines
of my remarks that in 1835 Quetelets book: "Sur l'homme et le dévelopment
de ses facultés, un essai de physique social" was published. Quetelet, who
taught astronomy and geodesy, was certainly influenced by Gauss and tried to
adapt statistical methods to problems belonging to social statistics. The most
important impetus came from statistical mechanics and the study of the
Brownian movement. Taking into account that the first attempts of Boltz-
mann to consider the theory of thermodynamics from a statistical point view
was made in 1866, one may say that the mathematicians needed more than
half a century to become interested in the corresponding mathematical
theories like stochastic processes and ergodic theory. In 1919 R. v. Mises still
favoured the idea that the calculus of probability was something like a "theo-
retische Naturwissenschaft". The stormy development of mathematical probability finally led to the set-theoretical axiomatization by Kolmogorov,
which has been the base of modern probability theory for the last 45 years.

The domain of applications of probability theory is steadily increasing. Control problems, econometrical concepts, computer science, decision theory, besides the traditional fields of applications like physics, biology and so on, have had an important impact on probability theory.

System analysis, computer science and mathematical logic have left their traces in a new axiomatic approach to probability which has been made quite recently by Kolmogorov, Martin Löf and Schnorr. The purpose of this approach is to narrow the gap between the mathematical foundation of probability and some of its applications.

Let me finally mention two important examples where inner-mathematical problems stimulated the creation of new mathematical branches. But the first steps toward these new concepts were carried out in the framework of concrete mathematical problems in other mathematical fields. It is very well known that in 1872 Cantor introduced the concept of a point set while studying the uniqueness of the development of a function in a trigonometrical series.

Another example concerns the origin of topology. When Euler found the celebrated polyhedra theorem, he had not in mind to lay the foundation of combinatorial topology but rather to give a systematic classification of polyhedras. He discovered that the trivial classification for plannar polyhedras where the number of edges is always equal to the number of vertices does not work for higher dimensions, and found the above-mentioned theorem.

And Riemann's deep considerations on the connectedness belong in a certain sense entirely to the theory of analytic cimplex functions.

The last thirty years has seen the development of big science not only in mathematics but in all natural sciences. A large part of sciences especially those of technical applications cooperates closely with the military-industrial complex. The great computer centers or the great centers of nuclear physics are similarly organized like the big industries and are frequently even of a multinational character. The socio-economical background of our highly industrialized world has of course also a heavy impact on the organization and the development of mathematics. The production of mathematical journals and books is dominated by a few mostly multinational publishers. The computer industry makes more and successful attempts to convince everybody that mathematics and computer science are identical and that pure mathematics does not serve a real purpose. Abstract mathematics is so to speak difficult to sell today and seems not to be able to lead to a quick useful reward and high profit rates. Several weeks ago a very well known mathematician gave a lecture in Vienna where he outlined a new theory. In a private discussion after the lecture when I indicated some possible applications of his theorems he was very interested because, as he said: "It is necessary today to give quickly applications of a new mathematical theory."

In conclusion I think that the mathematics of structures has reached a high degree of maturity. A tremendous wealth of material has been established by the efforts of the great mathematicians of the 20th century. Politicians, technocrats, military establishments and big industries have discovered that the methods and results of mathematics are important tools in automatization, in space-industry, in the aramament race and so on. These facts will lead to a fast increasing and overhelming interest in applied mathematics.

Arne Jensen

The Principle of Simplification, and Delay in the Creation and Use of Mathematical Disciplines

One thing we consider as a beauty within mathematics is the possibility, on a limited number of fundamentals and rules, to cover the present knowledge of mathematics. At the same time we create new branches on the mathematical tree, which in a simple and elegant way connect the different branches so that the total tree will be clear and simple.

But what is simple? What to one brain is a beautiful simplification is to another brain a disaster. He is not able to see what is behind this simplification, and how much it requires with respect to his precise knowledge about the rest of the tree in order to fully understand this beauty and its use. The result is that he is either not using it or misusing it, or, he may by pure chance just do the right thing. The natural sciences have gained a lot by applying the principle of simplifications. Deep understanding of their mechanism has been the result. Simplification has been a good guideline for the success of a science. But does that also always apply within mathematics? Mathematics is besides being an art also an instrument, and its use requires good information-bridges between the applications and mathematics. Mathematics is not only created by the good nursing of the mathematical tree or forest and by filling-in of obviously missing branches, but also by real world situations that create problems which require new thinking within mathematics, new branches or new fundamentals and rules. From mathematics we require not only the beauty from the simplification point of view, but also the beauty from the minimal number of mistakes and misuses point of view. Mathematics has got to fit into the surrounding world if you do not want it to end up as a sterile thing useful, only, to very few people. The rest of the people dare not enter into its use and have to go back in the literature in order to find some points of departure from the older times where they are able to hang on, instead of going to the refined tools of the new generations, requiring too much from them with respect to supplementary reading. In other words, we risk that we will get supplementary development within mathematics outside mathematics. It is not bad, one may argue, but, in fact, it is going to create delay in the use of new thinking. We have created a lot of new disciplines and new branches within mathematics which fit elegantly into the old hierarchical administrative system − the servant of which mathematics has always been. But is it fitting for today's and tomorrow's society to put so much emphasis on that part of the centralized governing system? It requires strong forces to get it carried through and very few people are qualified to do so, if it should not be misused. You may ask a specialist. Yes. But you cannot do that without a great risk that your problem might change a little, and often to such an extent that you do not really accept the answer. You may not have understood how much was placed in the assumptions you have accepted at the beginning of the work. Mathematics is a tool, and part of it you may automate. It is still so that the creation and the development of new disciplines, and also the use of disciplines already in existence, is dependent upon the information sphere between mathematics and its surroundings. Especially as far as the quality and ability of the brains able to understand and use it in their work are concerned. The biggest delays in the use of science and also mathematics are created by the pure fact that people do not know that somewhere someone knows something about their problems and their solutions. Man often does not understand himself, what he really wants to use. It requires at least that he should

be able to understand the most simple cases — and that is already a great re-
quirement to the building-up of mathematical disciplines. During the last
generation a lot of creative people have been cut off due to the modern development of mathematics and the changes which have taken place within the
teaching of mathematics. The positive result we might see in some generations. But presently we pay the bill for having cut down the number of people
able to apply it to ordinary problems which may not require the most refined
mathematics. When you create uncertainty in the mind of the user, you cut
off his use of mathematics and instead we get pure guess-work. That is not the
way to generate and develop new mathematical disciplines. The adaptation
process should be more carefully handled at the elementary level in the
future. The tree should also in the future be not only a beauty, but also
beautifully fit into the activities of the future society as an activity for a great
number of people assisted indirectly by the few refined specialists.

Bogdan Bojarski

The Possibilities of Mathematics and some
Anxieties in the Mathematical Community

The topic of this session is to discuss the factors inside and outside mathematics which are important in the generation and development of disciplines
in pure mathematics, during the most recent times. It is definitely very difficult, and perhaps it is a problem for special studies of historians and mathematicians or rather, historically inclined creative mathematicians, to detect
what can result from analysing historical experiences. Today we can only
express personal views, based on personal experience, about what the factors
in question are, and think more directly about what we should do in the
future to stimulate and facilitate the development of mathematics. I think
that there is a great anxiety in the mathematical communities all over the
world about a series of issues which influence the practice of mathematical

life, and we should, as I understand it, try to fix and collect these points and see what we can do with them in the nearest future.

We observe, when examining the process of mathematization of sciences, scientific activity and practical activity, the fact that the spreading use of computers contributes substantially to the practice of mathematization. There are, however, serious dangers in this extensive and spreading use of computers. Also from what was said here a little while ago by professor Schmetterer it can be seen that computer science and the industrial character of the activities of the computer centres contribute to creating the impression that mathematics on the whole is not very necessary. For instance the computer centres have a monopoly as to scientific methods which can be of use for the practice and which can contribute quickly to the development (economic, technical etc.). But, it is important to note that often the opinion is expressed that mathematics itself, pure mathematics, is not so much needed for this purpose.

It seems to me very important to propagate the understanding that mathematicians should participate in the very process of creating new scientific ideas and theories, in the endeavour of understanding the essential structure of the investigated phenomena, in the process of model construction. Only when participating in this model construction do mathematicians have reasonable possibilities to help to discover the analogies of the essential features of the model under consideration with well understood mathematical situations. I think that this imposes a very explicit duty on our mathematical communities of active intervention into the propagation of the possibilities of mathematics. There are very serious misunderstandings about what mathematics can do, about where it is essential. Some people tend to stress it as only a language, instead of stressing its properties as an essential tool for the investigation of nature, in penetrating its mysteries. It should be intensely propagated that this tool is not fixed, that it does not have any final form, that mathematics is capable of constant change, permanent improvement and perfection. This is in full correspondence with the purpose of better understanding nature and of extending the control of it. Very often mathematics is presented as something finished. Many people cannot understand that there is more to do in mathematics than has been achieved up till now, and even serious scientists sometimes have this sceptical inner conviction. Well, there is also a certain admiration of mathematics, but I have met situations when people at the bottom of their hearts mistrust the use of mathematics, verbally acknowledging its achievments. We could also give examples showing that mathematics has been used as a cover for pseudoscientific activities. This contributes to hampering the propagation and understanding of the value of mathematics.

So, I think that in the process of bridging the gap between active mathematicians, pure mathematicians, and other scientific communities, engineering, humanities, sociology, biology and so on, the mathematicians should take up very active positions. I know examples where mathematicians are satisfied with producing new theorems or new theories, very interesting, complicated, technically difficult, non-trivial indeed. Well, there is a hope that these results may prove useful some day, or will be taken up or needed by some other scientist, but the duties of the mathematicians are considered to end with their activity as producers of purely mathematical knowledge. Our meeting here expresses definitely the conviction that this should not be the case, and from my point of view I would like to stress that much more of the duty to show the relevance of mathematics in the process of any scientific investigation should be taken up by the mathematicians themselves, rather than by other scientists. We should actively intervene in the situation. If we don't do so we shall lose our position, and in some respect the positions of the pure mathematicians will be taken up by computers and people engaged in computer science etc. And this would create a situation which would be very difficult to improve and correct for a long time. I will just recall the opinion of the Polish mathematician S. Mazur, who said that every mathematician is better on any position and in any situation than any non-mathematician. Well, I do not agree with this statement, but I think that in the process of trying to penetrate nature, it is important that mathematicians intervene and participate from the very beginning, and not only when the scientist, engineers etc. think that they have a good or finished model of the situation and then bring this model to the mathematician for further treatment. It is in the process of formulating the model when the help and involvement of the mathematician is very important.

What I have just said is one side of the story: the involvement of mathematics in the process of creating new scientific ideas is not only useful for the "users" of mathematics. Many examples in the history of mathematics could be given when essentially new mathematical ideas arose from the efforts of mathematicians, physicists, engineers etc. to create scientific models of the phenomena of the surrounding world. The interaction of mathematics and other sciences, the applications of mathematics has always been an important factor in the development of new mathematical ideas. It is true that mathematics has its own logic of development, the interior problems of mathematics are very important, difficult and can occupy generatious of mathematicians. But history teaches us that in the long run it is of basic importance for mathematics to develop in close contact with other sciences. To preserve its position as a queen of science, mathematics has also to take the duties of the servant of sciences. This seems to be the logic of our time.

The other matter in which we, I think, should intervene very quickly, is the field of mathematical education. I do not know the situation all over the world, but I have some reasons to believe that there have been, at least in some countries, serious failures in the attempt to change the mathematical programme in elementary and high schools. This has resulted in diminishing interest in mathematical studies among young people, and perhaps we do not get the best, the most talented youngsters to mathematics any longer. They have grown interested in other kinds of scientific activities, and this seems to me to be a very serious problem. I think that this should also be one of the points of our discussion. The future of mathematics is inseparable from the state of teaching of mathematics at elementary and high school level. If we don't do something very quickly, it will be very difficult to improve things later.

Philip G. Kirmser

Comments on the Nature of Present and Future Success in Applied Mathematics

Human beings have always been driven to understand and explain their surroundings. Their attempts, although often laborious and sometimes ingenious, will be ever disappointing even though exciting ideas may be expressed in elegant language.

What is real is illusory and often difficult to decide. Recurring phenomena are explicable in different ways at different times. Descriptions are sometimes taken to be explanations; considered axioms often have no connection with reality; language occasionally creates reality instead of describing it; and diverse interpretations can be given for the same phenomena.

Why is this so?

Ultimately, all communication is based on meanings of basic words, defined by examples given in the context of the society one lives in. As societies change, understanding and description of reality shift. Societies having limited experience rarely formulate theories which seem reasonable to others. Science to one is magic to another. All language, including that of mathematics, has foundations in undefined concepts.

The major task of educational systems is to define and generate those common experiences which make communication possible. Universities must create access to these worthwhile defining encounters and probe the nature of reality by continuous experimentation. Exciting exchange must occur, for the paradox that no new ideas are communicable unless the recipient already understands them must be overcome.

Theory and experiment should always go together, for experimentation without theory is gadgeteering, and theory without experimentation is speculation.

It is here that we applied mathematicians have made our major contribution. We have developed and used general, logical languages to describe reality, both qualitatively and quantitatively, so that our descriptions could be examined for consistency, tested for accuracy, and used to discover unusual features of our world. It has not been easy. And it will not end, for the richness of the language developed makes many descriptions of the same phenomena possible. There are infinitely many theories which will fit any finite set of data exactly.

The value and success of mathematics are obvious. In every branch of science the most important theories are expressed in mathematical language.

Why are these theories used or accepted when multiple descriptions based on shaky concepts are possible?

Theories are accepted for various reasons — they may have elegance, simplicity, be psychologically attractive, or appear to be rational. Their proposers may be persuasive, prestigious, or influential - - or perhaps just persistent. Questions of correctness are not relevant, for every theory becomes incomplete or false when used to explain experiments or observations sufficiently removed from those used in its development. Theories are most valuable when they are simple enough to be used and accurate enough to make useful predictions for experiments not yet tried. The best theories are taken to be those which describe the greatest number of experiments, using the fewest parameters, which deal with phenomena of widespread popular interest. Simple theories, known to be incorrect, are often used in place of better, more complicated ones which yield equivalent results.

We are interested in the future of as well as the success of mathematics. How it will be viewed, and what directions the future will take, will not be much different from the judgments and attitudes which are generated by the activities of societies generally. A good way of predicting what the future will hold is to examine factors which made some branches of mathematics successful in the recent past, and to use these as a basis for extrapolation for promising developments which can be identified today. Consider, as one such branch, the field of statistics. It dates mostly from this century, its success is beyond question, and it has many of the characteristics of theories which were discussed above.

Is it correct? Who can tell. Is the world deterministic or probabilistic? Its basic concepts are shaky. The meaning of the word "random" is left either undefined or poorly defined in all textbooks used today.

It is persuasive. The words used in the field are a public relations expert's dream - - significant, highly significant, valid hypothesis, analysis of variance, random errors, etc.

It uses simple models. By using as few parameters as justified by the accuracy of the data at hand, it avoids all of the theoretical and practical difficulties brought on by striving for unproductive accuracy.

It is pyschologically appealing. In many applications it relieves us from the responsibility of our actions by removing our guilt. When bad things happen, they happen by chance, and the best we can do is to alter the odds a bit. And the chance that undeserved rewards are possible and do occur warms the human soul.

Statistics is applied to daily problems affecting every man. Since it is related to error analysis, approximation, and interpolation, it is certain that equally valid and successful deterministic but less popular descriptions could be made.

Will any mathematics of the future have the success that statistics has had to date?

I belive so. Conditions of the times have always had an effect on mathematics. *Newton* and *Leibniz* were probably pushed to invent calculus because they couldn't do the arithmetic required by difference equations. Now cheap computing machines, which have made extensive calculations possible, will cause an unbelievable spread of mathematical modeling and numerical analysis. Applications of discrete analysis are bound to become universal. Some of these are certain to drive mathematicians to invent new forms of analysis.

The existence of cheap computing machines and readily available software will spread numerical and logical analysis just as the development of phonographs spread the use and enjoyment of music with many similar results.

Mathematical modeling will be used to estimate the effects of social and political actions on our daily lives by providing accurate models of our economies, and perhaps, even our collective behaviors. Better decisions will be made by all of us because, as never before, accurate information will be available before the time for decisions has passed.

For the first time mathematics may even become dangerous, for it could become possible to decide which of two political systems is superior on rational grounds.

The practice of mathematics will increase but will become more diffuse and be carried on by many people not educated in traditional mathematics departments as they exist today.

And best of all, the need for good mathematicians will increase, for the intense and widespread use of mathematics to model all phenomena will require ever more careful scrutiny to separate good reality from more promising fiction. The future of applied mathematics is assured by its relevance to society.

Summary of the Discussion in Session 1.

The discussion in Session 1 touched upon three different points in connection with the theme of the session. These points were: "The influence of the real world upon the development of mathematics", "What is a real/good/important problem?", "Problems in recruiting mathematics students". These points were, however, interwoven in the discussion rather than treated as separate subquestions to the theme of the session. The following summary is, therefore, not in accordance with the chronology of the discussion. Instead, it presents a rearrangement which associates the ingredients of the various contributions with the three points.

The influence of the real world upon the development of mathematics.

It was stated that every resonable person will agree that socio-economic factors influence the development of every science, including mathematics, and that one can give many examples of this, from antiquity to the 19th century. On the other hand, it is very difficult for a person who lives in the period in question to detect the decisive factors in the development of a given discipline, not to speak of foreseeing possible effects of the factors operating at present. Of course it cannot be doubted that the economic boom after World War II with its climax in the sixties is tied up with the mushrooming of all sciences. An economic situation with ample resources available for science also stimulates an unrestricted development of pure mathematics, because people can do what they want to do, including producing results of minor importance. But when resources are scarce the situation is different.

Another contribution started by assuming that most of the participants in the Workshop would agree that pure research has a function, and that the reason why people had come together was an uneasiness about the way in which it functions. We have all been taught that mathematics produces new tools which are ready when they are to be applied, but we hardly know whether this doctrine actually holds good. Maybe the consideration of the old story about the working together of different branches in developing analysis might prove instructive. Although the roots of analysis should be found in a direct contact with the real world, analysis was not created by the mere existence of that contact. Nor were any of the branches, greek geometry and arithmetic, conic sections, archimedean volume calculation, the fertilization of these areas with algebra in the Renaissance or Kepler's and Cavalieri's application of archimedean methods, alone sufficient to create analysis. Not until problems in one of these branches were treated with methods from some of the others, so that many different areas melted together, was analysis created. The moral of this story is that maybe we should teach our students to treat problems in one branch with methods from other ones, perhaps not to produce publications but as a good exercise in treating problems from reality.

It was suggested making a distinction between micro-sociological and macro-sociological factors in the development of mathematics. Related to this is the question: to what extent, and how, is mathematics generated by empirical problems and, conversely, how is the mathematics developed applied to new empirical problems later? To illuminate the macro-sociological influence of society on the development of mathematics, attention was called to the interest of the big national and multinational corporations in applying mathematics, an interest strong enough to give rise to changes in research policy. Certain new areas of research are directly generated by multinational corporations (primarily in the electronics industry), e.g. quadripole theory, the cooperation of algebra and information theory, application and development of boolean algebra etc. Parallel to this one can see multinational corporations which attempt to infiltrate international scientific societies, in order to influence, for instance, elections to certain committees. This also has conse-quences for the control of important journals, financing of large international congresses etc. All this together affects research policy in mathematics, often without the individual mathematician knowing it.

Another aspect of this part of the discussion was touched upon by a contribution which found that the introductory remarks of Leopold Schmetterer took into account only to an insufficient extent the fact that the socio-economic context of mathematics also has ideological implications, e.g. as to social selection in school, acceptance of the social system etc. Leopold Schmetterer made it clear that ideological matters were included in his concept of socio-economic context.

In another contribution in this connection, it was claimed that whereas in earlier times (e.g. in Greek antiquity) ideological restrictions made a barrier for mathematical progress, such ideological restrictions no longer exist and this of course facilitates progress. On the other hand this seems to remove mathematics from reality because ideological restrictions can be considered as ties between mathematics and reality. In relation to this it was claimed that since mathematics always originates from problems in reality, no useless mathematics exists, and it is not only by chance that abstract mathematics can be applied at a later time. What would be a mistake would be to consider mathematics as merely a game. Probably it would be worthwhile to investigate (for instance as graduate-student research) why, when and how abstract mathematical theories have become applicable.

What is a real/good/important problem?

This discussion was initiated with reference to one of the questions in the informal questionnaire by Booss/Niss: What is it that makes a problem "real"?

It was suggested that we distinguish between a "real" and a "good" problem, and it was claimed that there exists a general agreement in the mathematical community that a lot of the problems dealt with in everyday mathematical research are not good problems, although it perhaps will turn out to be more difficult to find agreement on exactly what problems are bad problems. On the other hand there exist certain problems, the importance of which are not questioned by anybody, for example the Riemann-Conjecture. It would be valuable to produce a list, based on history, of good and bad mathematical problems, and a list of criteria for evaluating them. The view that a good mathematical problem overlaps different mathematical disciplines and maybe different sciences was put forward, and Hilbert's point of view, that a good mathematical problem can be explained to laymen, was supported.

Another participant mentioned that in mathematics a given object often obtains some sort of an objective, almost platonic, existence, in spite of its resulting from a purely formal construction. To the extent that we are dealing with such problems and properties of our objects that can be considered as independent of the formal theory in which the objects are studied, we are dealing with good as well as real problems. The Riemann-Conjecture is definitely a good and real problem in this sense; even if it has no immediate connection with reality it is fundamental for many mathematical areas. It is, however, by no means easy to determine what is a good problem and what is a pseudoscientific problem; compare the following quotation from a wellknown mathematician: "I do not know how to define my wife, but I am sure that if I see her, I shall recognize her".

From another quarter it was stated that we should consider mathematics as an insurance system against the unknown problems of the future, and that the best strategy for choosing problems therefore might appear to be a free choice by the research workers themselves, as it was said to be practised at the Bell Telephone Laboratories.

It was supposed that most mathematicians find it healthy to keep and develop an interplay between mathematics and its surroundings. People like Hilbert, von Neumann, Courant and others always stressed, that if mathematics became isolated from its sources in the real world, it would degenerate. If the palmtree becomes too tall and the top too far away from the earth, it will wither. Probably mathematicians will always respond to external factors if they are allowed to. In opposition to this we find the extreme point of view, that of Dieudonné's, that even if mathematics were detached from any other human endeavour, certain important results and big problems, generated by mathematics itself, would remain essential objects for study. In continuation, Dieudonné's mistake was characterized as being that he had not traced the origin of the big problems in a broader historical perspective. The Riemann-Roch-theorem, for instance, can be seen as a natural generalization of certain problems in theoretical physics at the time of its birth.

In addition to this, the traditional distinction between pure and applied mathematics was brought into the discussion and characterized as an unfortunate distinction which should be broken down. The task in this connection should be to create within the mathematical community the attitude that mathematics is a common effort of mankind in the programme of understanding and controlling nature. Such a changed attitude would keep mathematics in contact with reality and at the same time remove the basis of Dieudonné's position within the mathematical community.

It was further suggested operating with two different psychological types when talking about the relationship between mathematics and reality. The first type can work only under inspiration from problems in the real world, the other type does not need and does not use such an inspiration. It is necessary to take both aspects into account when educating mathematics students, where to too large an extent, it has been neglected to show how mathematical problems originate from reality.

With particular regard to the developing countries, it was stated as a problem that the mathematical socialization, which mathematics students from these countries receive when studying in the industrialized world, is strongly influenced by work which can be published in prestigious journals. In practice this will very often imply concentration on marginal or trivial problems from the surplus stock of leading mathematical circles. So, micro-sociological problems in the developed countries influence the macro-sociological problems in countries of the third world, because it is necessary for their development to direct the mathematical activity into work on real, good problems, the question only being: how?

This criticism against the publication system was also taken up in another contribution, in which it was found that this system has a decisive effect on the research and teaching activities of the mathematical institutions as well as on studies and motivation of students. The usual mathematical concentration on purely mathematical problems, oriented towards publication of papers which most probably will not be read by more than 10 persons, was pointed out as one of the reasons why, in proper applied research, a tendency towards employing mathematically inclined physicists rather than mathematicians can be seen, at least in some countries. This is so because physicists of this kind are much more used to work with *real*, real problems of the sort that interests the world which makes society tick, and which is also the world where the funds are. What is of interest to this real, real world is not only good, or real problems, but *important* problems, and for their treatment people are wanted to think ruthlessly, logically and purposefully, i.e. people who, if the situation requires experiments rather than symbols, take the consequences of that. We must encourage students to think in this broad sense, and this is particularly important for the 90%, who are not to become research workers in pure mathematics. A good applied mathematician is one who knows when to stop using symbols instead of using them abundantly.

In a following intervention these requirements were found to be relevant not only to applied mathematicians but also to pure mathematicians working with good problems, since good problems are never from the outset formalizable. For a closer analysis there is no principle difference between a good applied and a good pure mathematical problem.

As opposed to requirements of direct relevance of mathematical activities, the problem "by whom and how it is to be determined what is relevant" was pointed out, and a warning against using terms such as "useful", "applied" and the like as poetical invocations was given. Perhaps the use of such terms is due to a realisation that there exists more mathematics in society than in a direct sense is needed. The warning was also found in another contribution in which it was stated that we should not consider the legitimacy of mathematics as consisting only in doing service to man, although it is nice when this is possible. We should instead consider mathematics as an activity like eating, making love etc., and we should concentrate on creating activities which do not *hinder* good teaching and a unification of pure and applied mathematics, rather than expecting that we can *ensure* this.

Problems in recruiting mathematics students.

Taking its starting point in the worry about the diminished interest among young people in studying mathematics, and about the observation that mathematics perhaps no longer receives the most talented young people, a discussion concerning recruitment to mathematics took place.

To corroborate the claim that a change has in fact taken place, one of the participants referred to an American inquiry, based on 10 measurements. According to this inquiry, the extreme upper tail of the distribution formerly went into theoretical physics (and presumably to mathematics too), whereas it nowadays goes into biology. As another symptom, it was pointed out that more and more outstanding mathematicians leave mathematics in frustration at the lack of valuable social consequences of their activity. Instead, they have gone into medicine or politics. These symptoms should be taken seriously, and we have to ask ourselves: what is the impact of mathematics on society, what makes it worthwhile?

As a modification to the general picture, it was stated that the number of enthusiastic and talented students has hardly decreased in comparison with the situation of 25-50 years ago; what has happened is that the expansion of science and mathematics during the sixties has created an increment of students with other types of interests and future professions, for example in industry, computer science etc.

As to the question why mathematics formerly got the best students and why this is no longer so, the following answer was proposed: a. In earlier days mathematics teaching in school was much more based on experience and understanding than is the case today, where the instruction is so much concerned with formalism that a back lash has appeared. b. Many young people who earlier would have gone into mathematics, now go into computer science because it is popular and lucrative. c. In these years a general increased interest in social and humanistic, e.g. philosophical, questions can be found. With particular regard to the developing countries, it was mentioned that talented and seriously working students in these countries prefer to occupy themselves within fields, medicine for instance, that seem to be of more direct relevance to their societies, whereas mathematics appears as much more alienated to the big social problems in their countries. It was emphasized that, even if this attitude is understandable and respectable, it nevertheless produces problems, because the third world needs people with substantial mathematical abilities.

It was asked whether it was desirable at all that the best students go into mathematics. Wouldn't it be better if they went into politics, and shouldn't the mathematical community start to prepare itself to work with average students? This would also force mathematicians to take the communication problems of mathematics seriously into consideration.

Along the same track a warning was given against dealing with the problems of recruitment to mathematics as a question of increasing the membership of a club. A recruitment which serves only to produce research that can produce more research, often of marginal importance, is not in itself desirable. Rather one should concentrate on bringing mathematics to a larger public, to create "mathematical literacy".

From another quarter the danger of requiring immediate usefulness and the related possibility of misjudging what may have important consequences was pointed out.

2. Estimated Future Trends in the Development of Mathematics and of its Relations with the Non-Mathematical World

Maurice Kendall

Theoretical Statistics and the Real World

1. Theoretical statistics uses a great deal of mathematics but is not solely mathematical, except in a very broad sense. It is, for example, concerned very much with the logic of uncertain inference and although some of its problems can be referred to the theory of probability, others (e.g. the analysis of non-random samples or cluster analysis) can not.

2. It may be convenient if I classify the branches of mathematics into (1) those rarely or never used in statistics; (2) those used occasionally but not in depth; (3) those essential to the subject. One may add a fourth category, perhaps, (4) those which statisticians have had to invent or develop for themselves.

3. Category (1).
Branches of mathematics rarely or never used

Theory of Numbers
Topology
Projective Geometry
Differential Geometry and Tensor Calculus
Non-Euclidean Geometry
Mathematical Logic
Calculus of Variations
(and the applied branches such as Dynamics, Electricity and Magnetism, Heal
Light and Sound and Astronomy).

4. Category (2).
Those branches used occasionally but not in depth

Trigonometry including Spherical Trigonometry
n-Dimensional Geometry
Co-ordinate Geometry
Theory of Equations
Partial Differential Equations

5. Category (3).
Those branches essential to the subject

Analysis (Differential and Integral Calculus, Complex Variables and Infinite
Series)
Combinatorial Analysis
Matrix Theory
Spectrum Analysis
Special Functions (Gamma, Beta, Hypergeometric)
Probability, including Stochastic Processes

6. Category (4).
Special branches to the development of which statistics has contributed

Numerical Analysis
Sets of Stochastic Equations
Monte Carlo Methods
Cluster Analysis
Experimental Design
Sampling Theory
Time-Series

7. For some years statisticians have been concerned that the more recondite mathematical part of their subject is getting out of touch with reality. Continual attempts are being made to bring it down to earth, but not with great success. The advent of the electronic computer has not eased the situation, and in some respects has made it worse, in that a number of statistical routines can be plugged into the machine without a proper appreciation of what they mean, what are their limitations, and how the results are to be interpreted.

8. In the spirit of this conference I offer a few suggestions for ameliorating the position.

    1) Practising statisticians are often prevented from publishing or from writing text books, either because they work under Official Secrets Acts in Government Departments or because they work in business and have no time. There should be greater encouragement for *practising* statisticians (and practising mathematicians in general) to write of their experiences and to share in university teaching.

    2) Practising statisticians should be given an opportunity of describing their theoretical problems for mathematicians of the world to attack. In Britain we have just begun to publish an Encyclopedia of Ignorance, in which distinguished scientists describe their outstanding problems. Why not a conference or two on "What I don't know about mathematics"?

    3) Although mathematicians will, perhaps, not like this suggestion, I consider it a mistake to make the Department of Statistics in a University a part of either the Department of Economics or the Department of Mathematics. A review of the most productive statistical centres of the world will support this contention.

    4) Intermediate or even first year courses in mathematics should not strain after generality. Most of us, I suppose, have spent some time in our undergraduate days struggling with the illustrations that a continuous function does not necessarily have a derivative and functions of bounded variation. But did this ever matter to anybody except to the expert? There is a lot of dead wood taught in mathematics and enshrined in our text books. Who needs to learn all the different tests for the convergence of a series of positive real terms when one single test will handle them all? Do we really need to bother the average mathematician working in

the real world with the difference between Riemann and Lebesgue integration? Specialisms are for the specialists. Unfortunately reputation and credit often depends on specialisation.

9. In conclusion I should like to offer a few topics, thrown up by my own work, on which mathematicians may like to work.

1) If each of n objects bears a value of each of p variables, we may represent the situation with n points in a p-dimensional Euclidean space. For p>3 we cannot see this space. How do I define a cluster of points and how do I develop a mathematical expression to describe *shape?*

2) Rigorous mathematicians have suspected the human mind in its interpretation of diagrams – in my youth it was contemptuously described as the method of Pictures and Plausibility. Now is this not a flat contradiction of the way in which the mind works? In particular, if I have a set of n points in p dimensions, how do I define outliers?

3) Some problems can be solved by exhaustive enumeration on an electronic computer. The complexity of others implies that the machine time required increases factorially, even more than exponentially, with the dimensions of the problem. Suppose I have a set of m_1 male students who rank n subjects in order of preference, and another set of f_1 female students who do the same. How do I tell whether the men are more alike in preference than the women *within sampling limits?*

4) In multivariate distributions of probability the only distribution we can handle in mathematics is the multivariate normal (Gauss-Laplace). For others we should like to have distribution free tests, but unfortunately these depend on order and you cannot have an order in more than one dimension. What can the mathematician contribute to this problem?

10. I have reached the limit of length very rightly imposed by the organisers of the conference. I hope these comments may provoke discussion. Statisticians, after all, work in every field and are vitally concerned with the interface between their subject and the real world.

Salomon Klaczko

Cartesian Products and Factor Set Distributions as Models
of Mathematical Innovation

1. For many years a great quantity of theoretical work has been done on mathematical theorem proving (Herbrand, 1930, Gentzen, 1934). Since the ap-
pearance of digital computers several hundreds of mathematicians all over the
world have devoted themselves to the development of computer programs able to prove theorems without the intervention of man (an "older" state of the art
can be found in Laudet, 1970, Banerji/Mesarovic, 1970). This corresponds to
the last of four steps in thought, as suggested by Wallas (1926): 1. preparation, 2. incubation, 3. illumination and 4. verification.

Steps 2 and 3 correspond to what is called induction or creative thinking
(Lakatos, 1968, Watanabe, 1969, Ruzavin, 1977, Polya, 1954 and 1969). Our
aim is to discuss one procedure of inductive reasoning, able to serve as an aid
for mathematical innovation.

The basic instrument of this procedure occurs in mathematics in different
areas and unfortunately receives different names. In set theory it is known as
cartesian product, in abstract algebra and topology as direct product and in
linear algebra as vector product.

Among the applications of this instrument in computer science we can mention the so called Decision Tables (Pollack, 1971, McDaniel, 1970). An application to the theory of learning automata is the so called Learning Matrix
(Steinbuch, 1965). Even the Theory of Games uses this approach (von Neumann, Morgenstern, 1944).

A particularly interesting application for innovation purposes in research is
the method of the astronomer Fritz Zwickly called Morphological Box (Zwicky, 1957, 1958, 1971). The Zwicky approach became in the past decade a
standard method in the science of long-range or strategic forecasting (compare
for example the scientific US-journal, Technological Forecasting).

2. The above method can be applied to mathematics if we try to profit from
the axiomatic structure of this science. Let us consider first the fact that

axioms are properties of special sets. Given n properties, 2^n different combinations of the n properties may be possible. Take as an example a metric topology which can be generated in the following way

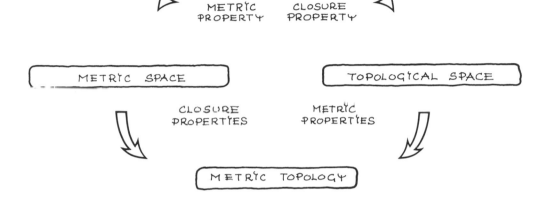

If we try to see it more precisely we will find the following properties

Closure Properties:

E. Single closure: $\bar{M} = \{a\} \Rightarrow a \in M \vee \{a\} = M$
F. Union closure: $\overline{M \cup N} = \bar{M} \cup \bar{N}$
G. Closure idempotence: $\bar{\bar{M}} = \bar{M}$
H. Closure distance: $\bar{M} = \{x \mid d(x,M) = 0\}$

Metric Properties:

A. Zero distance: $d(x,y) = 0 \Leftrightarrow x = y$
B. Symmetry: $d(x,y) = d(y,x)$
C. Triangularity: $d(x,y) + d(y,z) \geq d(x,z)$
D. Next neighbor: $d(x,M) = \min\limits_{y_i \in M} d(x,y_i)$

	Ø	A	B	C	D	AB	AC	AD	BC	BD	CD	ABC	ABD	ACD	BCD	ABCD
Ø												3				5
E																
F																
G																
EF																
EG																
FG																
EFG	1											4				
HEFG			2													

1: topology   3: metric   5: clusters
2: metr. topol.   4: metr. topol.

From the above 128 possibilities students of topology will find in their standard text books only the three concepts metric space, topological space and
metric topology; while students of statistics will find in their books the concepts of metric space and cluster space. Unnoticed by the greatest part of the
topologists during the last years such important non-metric mathematical spaces
appeared in statistics (being used in the theory of automatic classification) as
Quadratic Distance Cluster Analysis or as Multidimensional Scaling. It is
known (Pontriagin, 1957 § 9), that a topology (Axioms EFG) becomes a
metric space if axioms H and D are added. Thus, one of the tasks of the mathematician, given the above cartesian table, would be not only to answer
what meaningful non-trivial sets may be found in each one of the crossspoints,
but also to discover what crosspoints are equivalent to another and hence
redundant.

3. An exponential increase in difficulty arises however, if we try to incorpo-
rate a more complex structure than the one discussed above. Let us consider
the algebraic structures flowing together in the definition of an Abelian
Group.
                          − see the schema on the next side −

From the five properties of an Abelian Group, four are split into at least two
variants, generating 9 properties. Since the alternatives generated by splitting
are mutually excluding, we have no more $2^9 = 512$ but 30 possible combinations of properties. We introduced 13 of them, avoiding the different types of
so called Brand-Grupoids. This example shows that on this area far more work
has been done than in the example above.

However, a greater number of alternatives could have been substituted for the
quasi-associativity of the Moufang-Loop. For the axiom D (next neighbour)
any one of about 20 different agglomerative procedures of Cluster Analysis,
each one having strong consequences on the discussed space and on the consequences of their algorithmic implementation, could have been substituted.

4. Until now we have considered the properties or axioms of our mathematical
systems as given. But an important part of the axioms, as is the case in the
example of metric topologies, were not merely speculative inventions of
mathematicians. They arose from concrete tasks either from the real world or
from other mathematical disciplines. This is just the case with the different
variants from Axiom D, generated by specific classificatory needs in biology,
sociology or psychology.

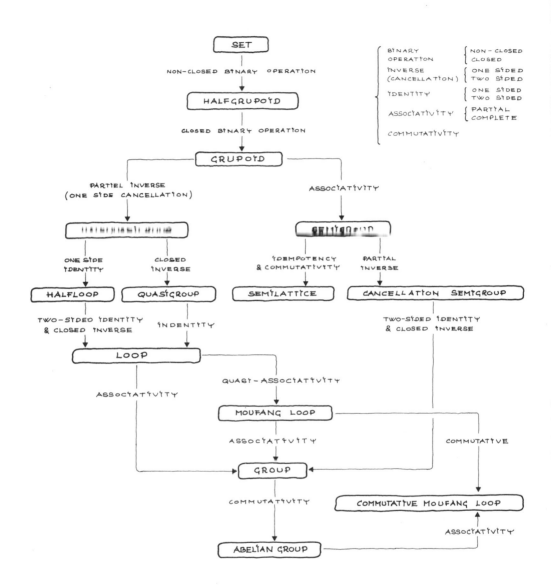

Algebraic structures flowing together in the definition of an Abelian Group.

The combination of the two examples — metric topology and algebraic structures —resulted until now mainly in the theory of topological groups (Pontriagin, 1957). The connection of each one of the stages (or properties) of Structure 1 and Structure 2 in a cartesian table would lead to a great number of non-formulated questions and problems. Taking one of the structures or a meaningful substructure (for example topological spaces) as a factor subset of the chosen properties, would render factor cosets in different areas. This last possibility implies the potential discovery of mathematical theories involving restricted areas of the cartesian table (e.g. a possible theory on topological groupoids or loops).

Wolfgang Haken

Some Thoughts on Mathematics in the Real World

"I don't understand how you can do research in mathematics; I thought that meanwhile everything was known there." I am quite used to hear this question being asked not only by people who have nothing to do with mathematics but also by engineering students after five semesters of mathematics at the university level. We seem to be very effective in keeping others mystified as to what we are doing and how far we have progressed. In order to explain the situation to everybody who is interested enough to ask for it I thought of the diagram below.   — see the diagram on the next side —

The statements at the levels 0,1,2,3, ... of the scale are probably all true but the difficulty of proving them increases significantly from step to step. Statement 0 does not really require a proof; however it requires a clear concept of what we mean by "number"; this level of sophistication may be considered the beginning of mathematics. The statement at Level 1 requires a genuine proof as was known to Euclid; it is a favorite demonstration example of a fact which is only accessible by mathematical proof. To prove the statement at Le-

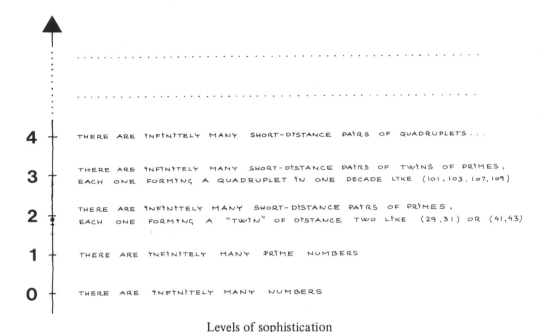

THERE ARE INFINITELY MANY SHORT-DISTANCE PAIRS OF QUADRUPLETS...

THERE ARE INFINITELY MANY SHORT-DISTANCE PAIRS OF TWINS OF PRIMES, EACH ONE FORMING A QUADRUPLET IN ONE DECADE LIKE (101, 103, 107, 109)

THERE ARE INFINITELY MANY SHORT-DISTANCE PAIRS OF PRIMES, EACH ONE FORMING A "TWIN" OF DISTANCE TWO LIKE (29, 31) OR (41, 43)

THERE ARE INFINITELY MANY PRIME NUMBERS

THERE ARE INFINITELY MANY NUMBERS

Levels of sophistication

vel 2 is a famous open problem of research in number theory; there we are. The interval from 1 to shortly below 2 depicts the progress made so far (of course, progress in many other directions of number theory branching out and being pushed forward with an effort of a million man-hours and a thousand research papers per year). Maybe at the level of 1.5 we may enter the famous prime number theorem. Using a magnifying glass one could see the more recent advances towards the twinprime conjecture at levels 1.8, 1.9, or even 1.95.

Is the above picture typical for all of mathematics or is it just some unimportant peculiarity of (one branch of) number theory? Gauss seemed to think while mathematics is the model for the exact sciences, number theory should be regarded a model for mathematics. What if he was right? — I am certainly prepared for objections. Indeed, everybody has the opportunity in his own research area to transform the "Level 2" to infinity and to deny that much interesting material would be beyond that. — Regarding the power and the limitations of mathematics one may seriously ask the question: do mathematicians themselves know the true state of affairs — at least approximately? (Do the termites know how their buildings look from the outside?)

The above questions are of some significance for the relations between mathematics and the real world. The classical recipe for attacking a scientific problem is to formulate the problem mathematically — whenever possible — and then solve the mathematical problem; of course, all mathematical problems which arise in such a natural way *can* be solved when eventually the proper tools are developed. But is this phantastic optimism still justified? If not then things become considerably more complicated. It does not really help to reduce a difficult scientific problem to an unsolvable mathematical problem. In many such cases it is appropriate to use a mixture of experimental and of mathematical methods — provided that the investigator knows both methods sufficiently well and does not care about the misgivings of those onlookers who know each only one of them. Frequently one sees applications of more questionable principles: Freely change the given problem by altering definitions and/or adding simplifying assumptions until the corresponding mathematical problem can be solved with moderate effort; then do not care about the alterations and claim to have solved the original problem. Conversely it may happen that the given problem can be solved by extremely simple mathematical methods; in this case be careful to create a more complicated mathematical formulation which calls for higher mathematics in order to make the work look more respectable.

One is tempted to distinguish between desirable and undesirable applications of mathematics according to whether the work mainly aims at clarifying or at confusing the issue.

What can we do to improve things? I suggest to rely on the objectivity of mathematics as its strong point. Whether a mathematical proof is correct can be determined by objective methods which (in most cases) do not depend on the arbitrary judgement of any individuals. This is great indeed, that the truth is above the arbitrariness of any person or interest group; this principle is worth extending over others areas of human activity as far as possible and we should take good care of it. We should; — but unfortunately, things look much less satisfactory if we consider the question whether a given mathematical result (assuming all proofs involved being correct) is important and interesting. Here the answer depends entirely on the judgement of the influential experts and not on any objective standards whatsoever. A mathematical result is important if and only if it pleases certain individuals; and that, of course, does not only change with time but depends on all sorts of other parameters too. This disease of unrestricted expert evaluation threatens to put us back into the middle ages and to disqualify mathematics as a model for the exact sciences. Here we should do something. But what?

It would help considerably if we had a certain core of carefully selected and clearly formulated open problems the importance of which is certified in such a way that it is not to be changed by re-evaluation at a later time. In particular, even if the wrong person solves the problem at the wrong time under the wrong circumstances and with the wrong methods (where "wrong" means "not being liked by the temporarily influential individuals") even then it remains an important problem. Such problems could then serve as objective tests for the merits and limitations of different methods and thus help to clarify controversial principal questions. I keep thinking that with some good will at least that much could be achieved.

Werner Böge

Technological Development and Effectivity of Mathematics

I believe, that the development of science and of production technologies and of computers will go on in the future as already in the past and that mathematics − pure and applied − will contribute to this development and will therefore continue to develop itself. This technological development will have many advantages for human life, but also it bears a lot of danger in itself, since science will perhaps one day make it possible to manipulate men or to construct still more dangerous weapons than before and many other unpleasant things. All this is only dangerous in connection with the fact that until now there have been no effective methods of democratic control and no effective methods for people as to how to agree about their different goals.

According to my opinion it lies within the responsibility of mathematicians − pure and applied − either to stop the technological and scientific development by stopping their own science, or to take care that this gap of missing methods for democratic agreement and control will be filled in a sufficient way. Actually this is the task of mathematicians and not the task of politicans, political or social scientists, psychologists or philosophers and so on − because of the following reasons. First of all, as I found out in recent years, the problem to find such methods is essentially a purely mathematical one, and a very difficult one. Secondly, only mathematicians are able to see that it is essentially a mathematical problem. Therefore, we cannot wait until somebody else asks us to attack this problem, because nobody will ask us, but we have to attack it by ourselves.

All countries pay a high amount for weapons. This is one of many examples of nonparetooptimality. That means that there are other possibilities, attainable by agreement, which everyone is better off with.[+] Such examples indicate that what happens is not governed by rational and effective methods of democratic agreement. Most people believe that this is due to the imperfect character of politicians and are angry with them, and they do not see that politicians are actually not able to do better because they do not have the appropriate methods. All the institutional methods they have and know about − both in western democracies and in communist countries − are combinations of the partial method of majority-vote. Some economists (i.e. Arrow and others) found out with some mathematical background that these methods cannot work, and they are aware of this methodological lack. But the mathematical background with which they tried and failed to attack the problem is too simple for fitting reality and to solve the problem.

That does not mean that every mathematican ought to attack it, but every mathematician ought to believe that his own investigations could one day be used for dangerous technologies and he therefore ought to take care that at least a sufficiently high percentage of other mathematicians attack the problem of unknown methods of democratic agreement, until it is solved in a sufficient manner.

The second point I want to talk about is much shorter and concerns the effectivity of mathematics. I believe that the organisational, technical and programming problems to be solved for the construction and use of computers, that do not compute in one or few central units, as they do nowadays, but that compute in all storage bits simulataneously, will not take too many years to solve. Almost all important problems that are solved on computers today, can be split into many very small problems, that can be solved independently by glueing the results together afterwards. These computers to be expected would solve these problems many powers of ten faster than computers nowadays with the same technical amount. I believe therefore that computer capacities will soon be large enough to do all pure mathematics much more effectively by computers than by human brains, and that by this the success of pure mathematics will be considerably accelerated and by this also the success of applied mathematics.

The essential bottle-neck will be the difficulty for pure mathematicians to learn how to tell computers to solve their very abstract problems. Therefore one ought already now to stimulate on an organisational level pure mathematicians to use computers to solve their problems. Of course one has to convince them that it will pay off soon, because most of them will not know about the very high computer capacities to be expected in the future.

X There are more less obvious but not less striking innerpolitical examples of this kind.

Summary of the Discussion in Session 2.

The topic of Session 2, the future of mathematics, was too broad to allow a discussion of detailed estimations and propositions regarding the concrete development of different mathematical branches. So it focused on the methodological problem of "objectivity" of the development of mathematics: "How to measure the relevance of an issue?". And, "Is contemporary experience sufficient for middle-range or even long-range predictions?" The debate was based on the unanimous conviction of the participants that mathematics can substantially contribute to man's governing of the real world, and that mathematics continues to make progress in this respect. So far, the discussion in Session 2 was closely related to the previous discussion in Session 1. More specific subquestions were: "Estimated future relations between "pure" and "applied" mathematics", "The possible use of computers for supporting — or substituting — human capacity in mathematical research", "Dependence of the future of mathematics on a widened mathematical training" (discussed more in detail in Session 3) and "Problems of the social responsibility of mathematicians".

The problem of "objectivity".

In the debate it turned out that many participants feel a "lack of objecitivity" concerning questions like:

How to measure the relevance and the prospective value of mathematical results?

Which criteria should be used in appointing people to vacant posts?

What is to be taught in mathematics education?

The urgent character of these questions was emphasized by participants with rather different views and experiences:

(I)   Under the hard competition nowadays seen in Western countries, a young mathematician may feel pressed by career considerations to work on problems of minor importance, where success might be easier than when dealing with more important problems and where results might better fit into the system of evaluation and aesthetical views held by the leading experts. What is a good mathematician? A way of evaluating, better than letters of personal recommendation, was demanded.

(II)   The above-mentioned lack of objective means to evaluate the work of a given person influences not only the careers and the pattern of qualifications of younger mathematicians. In practice many universities are now so short of funds and positions that they are (e.g. in some places in the U.K.) already planning how to replace all the pure mathematicians who retire in the 80's with statisticians, operations research people and computing file. Here it seems – in the absence of an objective analysis – that equally unsatisfactory and even anti-scientific policies are going to be adopted.

(III)   It was argued that the necessity of setting priorities for the allocation of funds and for the sponsoring of activities is neither a temporary or regional phenomenon, nor restricted to, for instance, the developed capitalistic countries in economic crisis, nor to developing countries with their strongly felt needs for reasonable allocation of scarce resources. There might be a *general* tendency towards "rationalization", also in the university system. The amount of open problems which are treatable from a methodological point of view will exceed the manpower at hand under all circumstances. Here mathematics may be said to possess a rather favourable position, as compared with more expensive sciences like physics. However, mathematics will also be confronted with the necessity of intensifying its own activities.

The reason for this pressure was seen not only in financial conditions, but rather in the very inherent process of mathematization itself, which is beginning to make mathematics applicable on a large scale, a fact which raises big expectations to mathematics in many non-mathematical quarters.

(IV) Internal mathematical progress and the enhanced role of mathematical methods in other sciences and in technology lead to a drastic expansion of mathematical training. At this point a longer debate about "dead wood", defined as concern with pathological situations, and the costs and risks connected with cutting off living wood, took place. It reflected the "lack of objectivity", the need for a more profound analysis of the dynamic interplay between the development of mathematical concepts and our understanding of real processes.

(V) It was not possible to draw common conclusions from this part of the discussion. On the one hand, it was seen as a test for the trustworthiness of mathematics whether we are able to establish objective procedures for "fair competition" between mathematical producers and between mathematical theories and methods. On the other hand, the historical character of mathematical theories was pointed out: reality should supply the criterion for relevance in the last instance, but mathematical modelling, like every scientific activity never constitutes a duplication of reality but rather an approximation. It might be justified, in this connection, to quote from the greetings by J. P. Kahane to the workshop: *"The only certitude is that science will grow and will move. It is interesting to grasp instantaneous tendencies, or to find where a new impulse is needed. But I fear that our experience is too short for a prediction, say, for 20 years, a fortiori, for deciding that there are 'open problems the importance of which is ... not to be changed by re-evaluation at a later time' (Haken). My feeling is that open problems are essential for the motion of mathematics, and they change according to this motion. In the interplay between problems, theorems, lemmas, theories, and definitions, how problems die and are forgotten is surprising at a first look. Actually it is quite natural".*

Estimated future relations between "pure" and "applied" mathematics.

Several participants expressed a sceptical view as to the possibility of distinguishing between "practical" and "purely theoretical" problems in mathematics. Instead of discussing which mathematical branches, theories and methods are superior in practical relevance, they suggested concentrating on a new, more conscious type of mathematician. This suggestion referred to experiences common to many mathematicians who have worked in industrial or other types of practical consulting: the changing nature of the one and same practical problem, and the well known phenomenon that many practical problems lead to mathematical problems, which are, in their first form, solvable neither by mathematicians nor computers. By taking into consideration features specific to the concrete situation, one may end up with a revised mathematical problem, containing more information and looking more complicated than the first one, but which may after all be solvable. So, if a problem of applied mathematics is formulated, it is a problem of "pure mathematics". And any part of mathematics may enter the scene at that stage.

In the discussion, there was a general agreement about the main lines of the "transform-ation of problems" described. From one quarter, however, the latent arbitrariness of this transformation was criticized for being idealistic and agnostic. It was also asked what percentage of mathematicians presently engaged in second rank research within pure mathematics are actually capable of carrying out the kind of cooperative work in question. To enable university mathematicians to play a part in assisting people in the engineering or science departments with their problems would require at least some additional expertise as well as drastically changed attitudes within the mathematical community towards applications.

The possible use of computers for supporting — or substituting — human capacity in mathematical research.

In their introductory remarks some of the panelists provoked a rather broad, and at some points very animated, debate on the prospective use of of computers within mathematics. It was suggested distinguishing between different objects of computerization of mathematical research activities:

(I)   It was reported that the problem of *representation of mathematical knowledge* has meanwhile been solved in principle. In view of the limitations in memory capacity and in speed of computation one has however to look for more comprehensible forms of representation (1).

(II)   A lot of work being done in the field of *verification of mathematical knowledge* with the aid of computers was referred to. As for the immediate future, strongly improved (combinations of) methods, concerning how to check given "proofs" or "ideas" and how to fill in the missing details by purely routine procedure, are to be expected (2).

---

1. M. Laudet, D. Lacombe, L. Nolin, M. Schuetzenberger (eds.), Symposium on automatic demonstra-tion, Versailles 1968. Heidelberg-New York-Westberlin 1970.

2. J. Herbrand, Badania nad teorja dowodu, Récherches sur la théorie de la démonstration. Prace Towarcyshva Naukowego Warszawskiego 3, 33. Warszawa 1930.

   G. Gentzen, Untersuchungen uber das logische Schliessen. Math. Zeitschrift 39 (1934-35), 176-210, 405-431. Reprinted in: M. E. Szabo (ed.), The collected papers of Gerhard Gentzen. Studies in logic and the foundation of mathematics. Amsterdam-London 1969.

   R. B. Banerji, M. D. Mesarovic (eds.), Theoretical approaches to non-numerial problem solving. Pro-ceedings of the IV Systems Symposium at Case Western Reserve University. Heidelberg-New York-Westberlin 1970.

   Selected Advance Papers of the 4.th Int. Conf. on Artificial Intelligence 1975, 2 volumes. Tbilisi 1977.

   H. Wang, Toward mechanical mathematics. IBM Journal for Research and Development 4 (1960). Reprinted in: H.W.: A survey of mathematical logic. Peking-Amsterdam 1963, pp. 224-268.

(III) As regards the *creation of mathematical knowledge* several approaches were mentioned, none of them, however, so far being completely implemented in computers. Random generation of ideas, symbolic manipulation, interactive graphical systems and learning robots are already in successful operation in industry. But computer-aided generation of new mathematical hypotheses will still need a long time, and as a minimum it will have to wait until we have determined in operational terms, what good mathematics really is — and found out how to tell it to the computer (3).

In the debate, several comments stressed that the importance of human activity in future mathematics will not decrease, even if supported by capable computers. It was argued that many problems will keep outside the capability of computers unless mathematicians are involved: The subjective aspects, the motivation for the activities undertaken by the individual mathematician, will be decisive for future progress within mathematics and for the realization of parts of mathematical research.

Dependence of the future of mathematics on a widened mathematical training.

If the trend of increasing interdisciplinarity continues, if mathematics becomes still more applicable, and so — in the last instance — more dependent on fruitful applications, mathematics as a science has no future independent of a progression of quality of mathematical training at all levels. This concern was expressed repeatedly in the discussion, and the still predominant underestimation within many mathematical circles of teaching was strongly criticised.

One crucial point seems to be the following dilemma. On the one hand it is nowadays both useless and impossible to teach everything that is known, on the other hand the opposite strategy, to concentrate only on what is important, demands highly intricate considerations.

Further the necessity of changing contents and rearranging curricula towards a better methodological training, concerning for instance how to apply mathematics, where to go and get the most relevant information etc., was claimed.

From another quarter it was reported that teaching "to order", i.e. developing and teaching specific training programmes for various needs, is considered an original scientific contribution in certain socialist countries.

3. G. Polya, Mathematics and plausible reasoning. Induction and analogy in mathematics (vol. 1), Patterns of plausible inference (vol. 2). Princeton 1954.

M. Boden, Artificial intelligence and natural man. London 1977.

P. Hajek, T. Havranek, Mechanizing hypothesis formation. Heidelberg-New York-Westberlin 1978.

D. A. Waterman, F. Hayes-Roth (eds.), Pattern directed inference systems. Proceedings of a Workshop held at Honolulu, Hawai (1977). New York 1978.

Problems of the social responsibility of mathematicians.

By the panelists as well as by other participants the existence of responsibility on the part of mathematicians was claimed — but questioned too. It was argued that every mathematician is quite familiar with situations where mathematics is used to prove completely wrong results starting from wrong axioms. So, mathematics is not responsible for the use and misuse made of it. Mathematics in itself does not influence reality, only the hands which use mathematics.

More directly, it was asked whether we could expect in the future to have to raise the question whether or not certain areas should be excluded from research on grounds similar to those discussed in connection with genetic engineering.

In suggesting an answer to this question one specific aspect of mathematics was pointed out: that theoretical results of mathematics can be used in many different connections. This makes it particularly difficult for a single research mathematician to find out whether his project is part of a larger framework.

Another participant asked whether mathematics as a whole could yield a model of rationality for other sciences and even for social life. But even in the face of possible and already existing misuses of mathematics the participants expressed their conviction of the fundamental importance, in the long run, of mathematics for the intellectual progress of man.

3. Difficulties and possibilities in Dissemination and Popularizing Mathematical Ideas, Methods and Techniques to Colleagues within Other Mathematical Fields and to the World at Large

Reinhard Selten

Accessibility of Mathematical Results

Researchers in other fields often find it extremely difficult to read mathematical papers and books which may contain valuable results useful for their own work. Partly this is due to the nature of the subject matter, but partly also to the style of presentation. Obviously something should be done in order to improve the situation.

Unfortunately the career opportunities of a research mathematician do not depend very much on the utility of his work for non-mathematicians. Scientific recognition is based on the judgment of fellow specialists, who do not sufficiently appreciate an effort to be understandable to outsiders.

Even if it appears to be very difficult to suggest effective ways to change the unfavorable academic incentive structure, some ideas may be worth trying.

It may be possible to find some source of financial support for special awards to those who make outstanding contributions to the improved accessibility of recent results. The amount of money involved need not be very great, but it must be substantial in order to emphasize the importance of the scientific achievement.

Another approach would be directed towards the reduction of the cost of supplying accessibility. Many mathematicians might be willing to change their style, if they were made aware of easily applicable rules which improve accessibility. Of course we do not have a set of such rules, and a research effort would be needed in order to find them. We do not even know what distinguishes well written mathematical text books from badly written ones. As far as I know, questions of this kind have not yet been investigated in a systematic empirical way.

There are several books on statistics which succeed extremely well in presenting advanced techniques to a broad public of non-mathematicians, who have to make use of statistical procedures. More than other fields of mathematical knowledge, statistics is user-oriented. The need for user-orientation will become stronger for other subjects, too, since more and more scientists in an increasing number of fields feel themselves confronted with the necessity to construct and to analyse mathematical models of empirical phenomena.

Mohammad El Tom

**The Proliferation and Popularization of Mathematical Results:
The Needs of Underdeveloped Countries**

I. I would like to view the proliferation and popularization of mathematical results in underdeveloped countries as a tool for the achievement of two related goals:

1. National (material and cultural) development
2. Promotion of mathematics

The second goal may be viewed as a proper subset of the first one if it is accepted that mathematics is necessary for development.

It is instructive to briefly indicate the different settings under which proliferation and popularization takes place in the industrially developed and underdeveloped countries.

In a typical industrialized country there exists a well-established and fully-fledged mathematical community possessing a reasonable reservoir of resources and a diversified and efficient communication system. Moreover, mathematics pervades, with a varying degree of sophistication almost all spheres of human activity. Thus there is a large pool of users whose interests cover a wide range of mathematics. All this makes the need for mathematics genuinely felt by society at large.

In contrast, the mathematical community of a typical underdeveloped country is both young and small (in many cases a community hardly exists). Mathematics is generally used at an elementary level and by a very limited and well-defined group of professionals (mostly engineers). Add to this a relatively high degree of illiteracy and you end up having what Professor B.F. Nebres of the Philippines aptly calls a "hostile environment" within which mathematicians work.

II.   I distinguish between three kinds of audience toward whom proliferation and popularization efforts may usefully be directed; each group having its own particular needs. These groups and their needs are as follows:
   A. Literate sections of the masses. What is needed at this level is to bring the power of mathematics to members of these sections (peasants, workers, nomads, fishermen, etc.) through the popularization of mathematical techniques which have as wide a range of applicability as possible to concrete problems which themselves ought to form the starting point in such efforts. What is certainly not needed are works in the spirit of L. Hogben's "Mathematics for the Million".
   B. Scientists (including mathematicians), professionals, senior officials and executives. The appreciation by members of this group of the beauty, power and limitations of mathematics obviously constitutes a most signi-

ficant step toward the realization of objectives 1 and 2 above. Besides familiar publications dealing with applications of mathematics to economics, biology, ect., I believe that there here is a need here for publications dealing with the use of mathematics in important developmental areas. This may take the form of an exposition of a specific area of mathematics with illustrative applications on problems arising in underdeveloped countries or a (team) report on a specific developmental problem.

C. Mathematicians. Besides publication of an interdisciplinary character referred to above, it is important to systematically make available for this group expository articles on recent major mathematical discoveries that span more than one area, i.e., results that build horizontal connections (e.g. Atiyah-Singer index theorem). Apart from their intrinsic educational value, such publications would certanly help mitigate the detrimental effects of the familiar problem of academic isolation.

III. It is quite evident that popularization efforts aimed toward the masses at large can only be efficiently carried out by local mathematicians (individuals, societies, study clubs, institutes, etc.). Moreover, besides publications, local mathematicians ought to make use of the hitherto almost untapped potential of educational technology (essentially, radio, TV, and film) if they are to realize a wider and fuller impact of their efforts.

While the needs of members of group B may be effectively met by cooperative efforts on national and/or regional levels utilizing "internal" resources, international cooperation would seem to be necessary for any reasonable satisfaction of the needs of group C.

IV. There are a number of problems that stand in the way of the realization of the ideas outlined above. Perhaps, the most important of these concern the availability of authors and publishers/producers of relevant material.

A typical mathematician in an underdeveloped country works in an academic institution which typically promotes its members according to traditional imported criteria of publications in international scientific journals. Thus it is evident that unless these institutions introduce important modifications in their promotions criteria, no serious and systematic efforts at popularization are likely to materialize; indeed, no worthwhile scholarly activity in science as a whole is likely to get off the ground.

The smallness of scientific (especially mathematical) communities of underdeveloped countries makes uneconomical the publication of material aimed at audiences B and C. An appreciable enlargment of the market is possible by aiming publications at regional groupings or even at all underdeveloped countries. I suspect that even in the latter case international publishers will not feel enthusiastic about entering the market. Moreover, a larger market introduces a language problem (English, French or Spanish? not to speak of national languages).

For a solution of these two and related problems, I propose the following: —
  (i) Academic institutions in underdeveloped countries should so modify their promotion criteria as to give adequate recognition to works on the proliferation and popularization of mathematics.
  (ii) The proposed "International Centre for Pure and Applied Mathematics and Development", if and when created, should make the proliferation and popularization of works aimed at third world scientific communities at large an integral and permanant part of their scientific activities.

V. To sum up, then, the achievement by underdeveloped countries of the related goals of total development and promotion of mathematics is ultimately conditional on the existence of large sections of the societies of these countries who are sufficiently appreciative of the power, limitations and beauty of mathematics and, indeed, of the scientific endeavour in general. The proliferation and popularization of mathematical results toward the masses, scientists and professionals is a powerful tool for the establishment of such appreciative sections of societies. While international cooperative efforts play an important role in the achievement of a wider and fuller impact of this tool, the role of local mathematicians remains decisive.

Ronald A. Scriven

The Communication of Mathematical Results to the Real World

The total number of scientific and mathematical papers published today is enormous and reflects more the need for research workers to establish their reputation in a particular field than the rate of advancement of real knowledge in that field. The chance that a given paper is read by more than a few people is small and this is particularly true in mathematics, as was shown in the survey by Woods and Fox (IMA Bulletin, pp 379-381, 1973). What is the chance, then, that academic papers in pure or applied mathematics are read by workers in the real world of applicable mathematics or vice versa? What is the chance of increasing this chance by creating a common forum to which workers of all colours in the mathematical spectrum will contribute and likewise receive based upon informativeness rather than respectability?

It has to be said at the outset that, human nature being what it is, the answer to both these questions is "very small, and much smaller than it ought to be". Having said that I want to mention briefly the work of two organizations in the UK of which I have first hand knowledge, whose aim is to increase contact and interest across the mathematical spectrum, particularly with a view to (i) increasing the involvement of academic mathematicians with real world problems, and (ii) motivating their students to do likewise.

First and foremost the "Institute of Mathematics and its Applications" was set up over a decade ago by leading British mathematicians with these very aims in mind. It currently has a membership of around 7000 mathematicians from all walks of life including the universities, schools, polytechnics, industry, commerce, government service, and so on. It has a small, hard-working, permanent administrative staff who service all the numerous activities of a professional Institute including the publishing of a learned multi-interest journal and a lighter, very popular, monthly "Bulletin", together with making arrangements for meetings and conferences on a wide variety of mathematical topics of interest to its diverse membership. As an officer of the Institute for several years with responsibility for the meetings and conference programme I may be forgiven for saying a few more words about this important part of the Institute's activities. Having noted the inefficiency with which published material in learned journals communicates "live" mathematics and developing techniques to the user it is extremely important that this gap should be filled by a lively and topical programme of meetings and conferences where the proceedings are published rapidly after the event. By this means current activity and new results are communicated to the user and the stifling requirements of respectability are avoided. Mathematical elegance is usually achieved after the real progress has been made and it is important in the real world that progress should be put before perfection. By way of example the meetings/conferences that the IMA has held recently have covered topics ranging from the flow of marine traffic to catastrophe theory and from financial investment to the flow of granular materials. Specialist groups within the Institute on numerical analysis, control theory, and environmental mathematics have been formed to foster contacts and communication within these important applications areas and further groups will be formed as interest in new areas increases.

A second important but smaller development has been the formation of Study Groups with Industry at Oxford University Mathematical Institute. These meet once a year and mathematicians from industry or commerce with problems involving the analytic or numerical solution of differential equations of all types spend a week at Oxford discussing their problems with the academic staff. Staff and postgraduate students are allocated to problems according to interest and after the residential workshop is over follow up is done on a personal basis until satisfactory solutions are found. In this way interesting problems are brought to the notice of the staff and industrial representatives not only receive help with their problems but have a valuable mini-sabbatical in congenial surroundings.

Finally, I would like to return to my first point regarding the concentration of mathematical research activity in areas which are deemed to be respectable and publishable even when they have little if anything to do with the real world that provides the financial wherewithal for this activity to continue. Perpetuation of this activity has its influence on the research and motivation of postgraduates which in turn affects the training of graduates and the content of graduate courses and this influence percolates down through the whole educational system into the schools, affecting the next generation of potential mathematicians. In particular, able pupils and students may be put off mathematics for life by being presented with too much abstract mathematics too early in their careers. A more balanced diet is required in the formative years when the majority can readily appreciate the power of intuitive ideas and elementary applicable mathematics. Even arithmetic proficiency in the young school leaver would be a step forward in this present day and age. We seem to forget too readily that the strides made by the great mathematicians of the past like Newton and Gauss were motivated by a personal interest in solving the real world problems of their time rather than an interest in studying mathematical structures per se. It is surely more important for mathematical educators in general to follow this lead and motivate the young into using mathematics to study all aspects of the world they see around them rather than to tread the narrow road of current academic activity.

I have mentioned two developments in the UK which are aimed at closing the gap between academic and real world interests in mathematics. No doubt there are more individual initiatives within university departments which deserve more publicity and encouragement. I have also made comments on the way academic attitudes and activity at the research level have adverse effects throughout the whole educational process. Much needs to be done and attitudes need to change on both national and international scales if these problems are to be solved in spite of professional selfinterest. I hope that the efforts of the Roskilde workshop is an international initiative that will be continued long after the participants disperse.

Boris V. Gnedenko

Popularisation of Mathematics, Mathematical Ideas and Results in the USSR

1. Mathematics is everywhere in our knowledge of the real world, and in the practical life of modern society occupies an exceptional place. However, very often, many persons for whom mathematics is essential for scientific or for practical activity are badly informed about its possibilities, ideas and results.

2. Now there arises a necessity to popularise mathematical knowledge, to demonstrate its efficacy for solving practical problems. Moreover this propagat-

ion must concern not only pupils' teachers, but also medical doctors, biologists, engineers, economists, specialists in agriculture and workers. This last category of recipient is very important, in sofar as the modern worker not only executes a monotonous sequence of actions, but takes some basic decisions for control of technological processes or for quality control.

3. Naturally the propagation of mathematics must touch not only applied aspects but also general ideas, tendencies of development of mathematics, its history and philosophical problems.

4. Each group of recipients needs a special approach. It is impossible to present the same question by the same method for schoolboys and engineers It is necessary to take into account the interests and intellectual level of the recipients.

5. During the last forty years I have had to give many lectures for teachers and workers, for university students and engineers, for soldiers and the general public. I change not only the style of exposition but also the titles of the lectures. For example, the lecture "The place of mathematics in knowledge of the real world" I give for students and for engineers, but for soldiers and workers I give another name "Why is it necessary to develop mathematics?" I must add that the contents of the lectures were also very different: examples, general ideas, not solving problems and so on.

6. The propagation of mathematical knowledge is carried out in my country in several different ways:
   a) Universities organize public lectures,
   b) Universities and the schools organize mathematical circles, lectures and mathematical olympiads for schoolchildren,
   c) The society Znanie (Knowledge) organizes separate lectures and cycles of lectures for specialized audiences and for all needs in different cities and in the country,
   d) The society Znanie and the publishing house "Nauka" (Science) publish several series of booklets. Individual popular books are published by many publishing houses — Znanie, Prosvesthenie (Enlightenment), . . .

7. The series of booklets of "Science" have the name "A library for school mathematics circles", that of the society Znanie consists of twelve little books (64 pages). The price of one such book is 11 copecks, and about 50.000 are

printed. Some examples are:
    V.G. Boltiansky, Optimal control,
    V.I. Levine, Ramanujan,
    B.V. Gnedenko, Some ideas in queuing theory,
    N. Bourbaki, Architecture of mathematics,
    A.N. Kolmogorov, S.L. Sobolev and other, New ideas in mathematical
    education,
    I.M. Iaglom, Mathematics and the real world.

8. I think it is well timed to organize international series of booklets for popularisation of mathematics, its ideas, its connection with the real world and its history. Historical booklets must be in general not biographical in character, but on the history of mathematical ideas and mathematical creation.

Avi Bajpai

An Editor's View

In a modern technological society the role of mathematics as a subject in its own right as well as a support discipline is bound to be a crucial one. We all know of many instances where children have shied away from mathematics during their primary or early secondary education. Lack of interest in mathematics prompts the children to choose non-mathematical subjects in their schooling which naturally affects their choice in further and higher education. The problem of children not opting for mathematics is often found in developed countries. It is, however, much more acute in the developing countries which are competing with technologically advanced countries and are losing out in their serious attempts to raise the standard of living of their people.

My own experience and background has often led me to compare the situation with regard to mathematical education in the developed as well as developing countries. What has struck me most is the shortage of suitably qualified mathematicians who have first hand experience in how to "apply" mathematics to "real" problems. Many are even unaware of the sources from which they could get some background information on applications of mathematics in science and technology. There is obviously an urgent need for mathematics to be made relevant, applicable, meaningful and most of all, interesting and enjoyable to school children. If the children are fascinated by the subject for whatever reasons, the task of those who teach them becomes that much easier.

The third session at this Conference is concerned with proliferation and popularisation of mathematics. I have no doubt that we must make mathematics popular within the mathematics community and very much so with the "users" of mathematics. I strongly hold the view that any attempt to achieve this objective is worthwhile. We did this by starting, with the collaboration of Professor W.T. Martin of Massachusetts Institute of Technology, the *"International Journal of Mathematical Education in Science and Technology"* in 1970. It is now in its ninth year and has an international Advisory Editorial Board, some of whom are mathematicians but many are "users" of mathematics. They help in formulating the policy of the Journal, which is to benefit the teachers and users of mathematics in an inter-disciplinary context. To amplify my point I quote below the *Aims and Scope* of the Journal.

"Mathematics is pervading every study and technique in our modern world, bringing ever more sharply into focus the responsibilities laid upon those whose task it is to teach it. Most prominent among these is the difficulty of presenting an inter-disciplinary approach so that one professional group may benefit from the experience of others.

This journal exists to provide a medium by which a wide range of experience in mathematical education can be presented, assimilated and eventually adapted to everyday needs in schools, colleges, polytechnics, universities, industry and commerce. Contributions will be welcomed from teachers and users of mathematics at all levels on the contents of syllabuses and methods of presentation. Mathematical models arising from real situations, the use of computers, new teaching aids and techniques will also form an imprtant feature. Discussion will be encouraged on methods of widening applications throughout science and technology.

The need for communication between teacher and user will be emphasized, and reports of relevant conferences and meetings will be included. The international experience collected in these pages will, it is hoped, provoke a discussion bringing clarity to mathematical education and a better understanding of mathematical potentialities in all disciplines."

This poses two very important questions. Firstly, what means should be adopted by the leaders of the mathematics community, some of whom are gathered here in this Conference, to make it possible for a large body of teachers teaching at various levels and for students to benefit from what already exists. I do not believe that there is a need for more journals to be started at this juncture. That certainly would be "proliferation". Instead, what should be considered very seriously is how to extract the useful information that exists in current journals and circulate it to wider audiences in all parts of the world at an economic cost. Secondly, most people comment that mathematics books are difficult to read and understand, especially by the "user". We need mathematics books written in simple language with motivational examples for the type of user they are aimed at and published at an economic price. The price is an extremely important factor for developing countries, which often cannot afford the foreign exchange required for buying good books published in developed countries. If publishers were willing to co-operate, they could commission authors from the developing regions to collaborate with authors from developed countries to write such books. The books then could be printed and published very cheaply in the developing countries.

In conclusion, I strongly recommend to the national and international committees on mathematics instruction, particularly the ICME, to determine ways and means of spreading much useful and relevant information on mathematical education, already available in existing journals. Furthermore, positive steps should be taken to produce cheaply short monographs on mathematical topics with particular relevance to the needs of the "user", written in collaboration by authors from developing and developed countries.

Summary of the Discussion in Session 3.

In the discussion different points within a relatively broad spectrum of topics were commented upon. These points were mixed up with each other, which inspired some of the participants during the session to suggest various distinctions in order to categorize the topics touched upon and to structure the discussion at large. Although the impact of these suggestions on the course of the discussion was not in reality very marked, the following resumé of the discussion to some extent, but not completely, reflects categories suggested during the session. These categories are: "Dissemination within the developed world of mathematics to non-mathematical users, in industry, in other sciences etc.", "Dissemination of mathematics to developing countries and to underdeveloped regions of developed countries" and "Dissemination of mathematics to children and students".

Other categories were also suggested but were not, or only periferically, treated in the discussion: dissemination of mathematics within one subject to mathematicians working in other areas of mathematics, dissemination of mathematics through mass media, dissemination of mathematics to politicians and decision makers. It was stressed by one of the participants that the goals related to the different categories of dissemination should be made clear, and that these goals should not be expected to be the same or to imply the same consequences.

The dissemination within the developed world of mathematics to non-mathematical users, in industry, in other sciences etc.

This section of the discussion took its starting point in the panel contributions by Reinhard Selten, Ronald Scriven and Boris Gnedenko.

On the first point within this section the panel was asked what could be done to disseminate mathematics to potential users who are not interested in mathematics for its own sake and are often even hostile to mathematics. Selten found the most urgent task to lie in bringing mathematics into a form attainable without an unreasonable effort to those users who already want it. Scriven answered that according to his experiences with engineers, chemists etc., users tend not to apply mathematics even if one tries to encourage them, bring them to meetings and the like. It seems that there exists a level of confidence towards mathematics, varying from person to person, which has to be surpassed if the person is to take up mathematical tools deliberately. Gnedenko agreed on the necessity of investing some effort in showing users how mathematics can be of use to them. In Moscow University supplementary education in mathematics through special three-year-courses has been offered for 15 years to engineers, many of whom have shown much interest in taking up the offer, and now many engineers use mathematical methods in their technical work.

One participant warned against the danger of exaggerating the eagerness to convince non-mathematicians that mathematicians can help them in solving their problems. In many situations they would be happier, if they could solve them without using mathematics.

On a slightly different track of the discussion a participant from Latin America reported on experiences with building up in his country a new institute of mathematics, which aimed at meeting regional needs and demands of development, closer to real world problems than is seen in connection with traditional mathematical institutes. In order to fulfil these aims the institute had appointed non-mathematicians (engineers, agricultural and medical scientists and so on) as staff members. This was based on the philosophy that if mathematicians undertake applied mathematics, they produce *theoretical* applied mathematics rather than involving themselves directly in problems of reality. This difficulty as well as the answer suggested to it was considered to be the same in both developing and developed countries.

Similar experiences with employing non-mathematicians in mathematics institutes were gained with engineers at a department in a European country.

From another quarter a participant from Eastern Europe stressed the same problems and aims as were reported from Latin America, but pointed to a somewhat opposite kind of solution, tried out with success in his country. There a group of mathematics professors worked for two years in industry in collaboration with engineers and physicits who already knew a good deal of mathematics and were rather sceptical as to the possibility of obtaining further real contributions from university mathematicians. In half a year, however, they changed their opinions and even wished to receive mathematic students in their factories. Now in many sectors so-called application groups, with about ten mathematicians working on industrial problems, have been established. These groups do not ask "what mathematical problems do you have?", but "what concrete problems do you have?". It has turned out, in addition, that these concrete problems often lead to very interesting mathematical problems, which can be treated more thoroughly by university mathematicians. And this in turn has also had a positive impact on the education of mathematicians.

It was reported by another participant that similar activities have successfully taken place at a university in the U.K. on the initiative of the National Science Council, which circulated the idea to all universities in the country, of which only two responded. A study group between mathematicians and industry has now for 5-6 years considered mathematical problems arising in industrial contexts and has selected about five of them for closer investigation, where people from industry spend a week in the milieu of university mathematics discussing the problems with interested staff members, trying to formulate these problems differently etc., and with PhD-students allocated to them.

Other contributions along the same lines reported on similar experiences with collaboration of mathematicians and non-mathematicians. It was stressed that such initiatives should not be limited to industry; parallel problems and parallel activities are just as relevant when dealing with other aspects of dissemination of mathematics, at governmental level in administration, planning, resource allocation, and in connection with other sciences which could gain much help from mathematicians working in groups with advanced scientists.

Another participant found that mathematicians not working in universities were forgotten in the discussion, although they may be contributing to the process of dissemination and popularizing mathematics. How to arrange and keep contacts between universities and such mathematicians, working in industry and the like, once they have left the universities? One problem here is that many companies are probably not willing to give mathematicians employed by them sufficient time to participate in such contacts. Another problem is that university mathematicians do not know very well what could be appealing to mathematicians outside universities.

Dissemination of mathematics to developing countries and to underdeveloped regions of developed countries.

That part of the discussion which is categorized under this heading was primarily initiated by the panel contribution by Mohammad El Tom.

At the beginning of the discussion it was asked if there exist any studies on the correlation between the mathematical level of a given country and the state of economic development of that country. No answers to this question, with particular regard to mathematics, could be given by the panelists or the audience, only studies correlating general human/scientific capital and economic development seem to exist.

One participant found that perhaps we should direct ourselves only to developed countries, because a major problem is that in developing countries the governments, for obvious reasons, are much more concerned with raising the standard of living than with developing mathematics, so that the boundary conditions for the discussion are widely different as to developing and developed countries.

This contribution was strongly opposed by Mohammad El Tom, who emphasized that he had not asked people to direct some of their efforts to work with problems of developing countries. On the contrary he found it necessary for these countries to become self-reliant also in this respect, but since it is hard to obtain such a self-reliance and since many problems with the functioning of mathematics in society lie within the intersection of concern of the mathematical community at large, he could not accept that the problems of developing countries be kept out of the discussion.

Another participant suggested that one of the reasons for the lack of application of mathematics in developing countries could be found in the absence of industry producing technology, so that a demand for mathematics and mathematicians is not very strongly raised.

From another quarter it was stated that the problems of disseminating mathematics to developing countries have analogous counterparts in the problems of disseminating mathematics to underdeveloped regions or underprivileged groups in developed countries, for instance in USA. These problems should be seriously faced, and initiatives should be taken to start tackling them.

Along a different line in this part of the session, and with relations to the first part, some conditions for disseminating mathematics to various receiver groups were pointed out.

As one such condition, the importance of which was supported by referring to the process of acceptance of ideas and methods from Muslim mathematics in the mathematical community of the Middle Ages in Europe, the following was mentioned: the crucial role of local scholars who digested and transformed the new ideas into a form compatible with the existing knowledge and pattern of thought. Not until this transformation had taken place, were the new ideas accepted in the learned world at large. It was found that this condition holds for present times as well, and for both developed and developing countries.

This point of view was further elaborated by another participant, who emphasized the necessity of focussing on the type of transformation needed in the process of dissemination in order to recognize its character. One observation could be made already, that is that things do not move by themselves, something serious has to be done, if the process of transformation is to take place at all.

Dissemination of mathematics to children and students.

The starting point for this last section of the discussion in Session 3 was found in the panel contribution by Avi Bajpai.

From the audience it was asked by what objective methods it could be measured that the level of mathematical ability and proficiency of school children had actually gone down, as stated for India. The fact that parents and teachers are worried does not suffice for a proof; parents and teachers have always been worried.

Avi Bajpai answered that with the introduction of modern mathematics in school a type of mathematics which neither appeals to parents nor to teachers (because they are unable to explain the modern methods to laymen) had been introduced. He found it sufficiently established that a lack of numeracy amongst children exists, and that this causes great concern, with parents being afraid of a retardation of the career possibilities of their children, if this inadequacy remains.

Another participant supported the observations mentioned by referring to an experiment with engineering students in subjects closely related to mathematics. In this experiment students were given ten years old exams, with only dates changed, and they managed considerably worse than the student ten years ago, measured by marks and passing rates.

The relevance of this experiment for the conclusions drawn was doubted by several participants. One found the results not to be surprising at all when the change of curriculum is taken into consideration. Another one stressed learning as a social process, for which evaluation is extremely difficult.

Changing the line of discussion the following point of view was introduced: we should not ask for as much mathematics and for as many mathematicians as possible. We should not want anyone who could become a mathematician to become one, just as we do not want anybody who could become a carpenter to become a carpenter. There is no risk that a Gauss would be lost in our educational systems.

To this it was objected that the problem is not only that of losing potential future mathematicians but rather frightening young people away from taking other subjects in which mathematics play a part.

In another contribution it was stated that the capacity of acquiring mathematics is not a problem of gifts but of the total history in a social context of the individual, and on this background it would be perfectly possible to lose a Gauss in our school systems.

This was agreed upon by a different participant, who brought the considerations further in saying that many people, the names of which we could never know, had never had a chance to acquire both the opportunity, the material basis and the motivation for mathematical training. An example, without names, was given of a leading mathematician who was a semiliterate peasant until he got the opportunity to get a special training.

-o0o-

Outside the three main lines of the discussion summarized above, other comments on particular issues were given throughout the session. Among these were the desirability, advocated by one of the participants, or the non-desirability to let people studying mathematics, whether with a view to taking up a mathematical profession or not, come into contact with open problems of mathematics.

Another issue was the problem of producing good books and journals for mathematicians and for users of mathematics, for developed as well as for developing countries, at a sufficiently low price. It was suggested that such books could be produced in developing countries with cheap labour and then exported to the developed countries. This was refused by another participant, both because of political reasons and because of the distinct needs of the developing countries, which make production of common books unreasonable.

4. Discussion and Initiation of Concrete Initiatives in Continuation of the Work Done in Session 1–3

Summary of the Discussion in Session 4.

A panel consisting of Ubiratan d'Ambrosio, Lothar Budach, Geoffrey Howson and Lee Lorch opened the last Session, which was devoted to an exchange of ideas, concerning how to formulate elements of a joint policy and which concrete initiatives should be taken towards this end. It was generally agreed not to draw too farreaching conclusions from the debate of the workshop, because of the necessarily introductory nature of the discussions. It was, however, felt that the multifaceted experiences transmitted by people from many different countries and from many different fields could serve as a source of ideas and as part of a basis for future work.

Some kinds of requested activities.

Among the many proposals, two kinds of activities seemed to be most firmly supported by the participants:

(A) Mathematicians and mathematical societies should work to improve channels of communication with individuals, groups and institutions that can advantageously contribute to the application of mathematics for the benefit of humanity and from which mathematics can derive new ideas, directions and problems.

(B) One has to take into account the new global character of mathematics and to cultivate cooperation between various parts of the world for the satisfaction of cultural and developmental needs (x).

Several means of supporting such activities were discussed:

1. The problem of *incentives* was mentioned several times: financial incentives and in-centives of professional recognition. Some participants warned against drastic administra-tive changes, because of the danger of introducing present antiscientific tendencies.

2. Changes in the *career pattern* were proposed, with particular reference to experiences from some countries with more "coming and going" between universities, industry and government institutions.

3. A general change in *climate* within the mathematical community, concerning the development of the social involvement of mathematicians and mathematics institutions, was considered highly desirable.

4. In that connection, more theoretical work on *"knowledge about knowledge"* was considered desirable. In other words, what are the concrete conditions and needs of popularization and acceptance and of development and application of mathematics?

5. Finally, *the role of international and national organisations as well as of local institu-tions and communities* was touched upon. Some differences between the objective needs of our time and the way in which most of these institutions still function were observed.

The following organizational means, ideas, and considerations were discussed in more detail:

The character of the international conferences.

The character of international conferences on mathematics, and the International Conference of Mathematicians in particular, was touched upon. Many participants found that international conferences have an increasing importance as places of professional contact.

As regards the International Congress of Mathematicians (ICM), the work done by the Consultative Committee of the International Mathematical Union (IMU) and the Panels

---

(x)   Motions of similar contents were passed at the meeting "Mathematics and Society", held at the
        ICM 78, and a meeting "Mathematics and Development", held at Bordeaux in November 1978,
        respectively.

for the single sections were recognized. But it was widely questioned whether the amount of time and energy, of ideas and initiative spent on the preparation of the ICM was reasonably invested, when considering "the arrogant narrowness" as a participant put it, of a programme directed to several thousand mathematicians from all parts of the world coming together in one place for ten days, not to speak of the fact that very many mathematicians, almost all statisticians, engineers and other users, and teachers of mathematics have given up attending the ICM. It was argued that the traditional way of preparation by small anonymous and mostly selfrecruiting circles might be still very efficient for the organisation of research seminars in limited areas. In order to make the ICM a true expression of the mathematical life on earth, a demand for a much broader, more qualified debate on the concept and performance of next ICM's was raised. It was recommended that national and local mathematical communities should be included in the preparatory work of the ICM's.

Some suggestions were made:

1. Truly *representative survey lectures* should be given, and speakers should be selected and invited with regard to their capability of grasping and expressing the main trends and the bearing ideas in their fields.

2. A more careful and balanced *division of the whole body of mathematics* into subfields was recommended and a more representative *review of the applications of mathematics* was demanded. Some statistics on the total distribution of invited lectures to the ICM 78, in Helsinki, were presented:

- algebra and geometry .... 48 talks
- analysis (with quantum dynamics and relativity) .... 49 talks
- discrete mathematics and "computer science" (one of the speakers invited
  to this section confessed not to have had computer experience exceeding
  half a year) .... 6 talks
- mathematics and social sciences .... 2 talks
- history and education .... 2 talks

It was stated that the gap, shown by these statistics, between the classical mathematical disciplines and areas which have grown up in the last twenty years cannot be satisfactorily filled by parallel activities alone, e.g. of the Bernoulli Society for Mathematical Statistics and Probability, nor by the diverse engineering- and operations research- and other mathematics user's societies such as the International Federation of Information Processing (IFIP). In the face of the accellerating specialisation and diversification of mathematical activities, the main responsibility of the International Mathematical Union (IMU) was pointed out to be to *defend the unity and the progressive potential of mathematics* not by almost excluding applicational aspects but by incorporating the theoretical problems connected with the application of mathematics.

3. Some concrete proposals concerning the problem of attracting the interest of the mathematical community to the *interplay between mathematics and the real world* were put forward:

(I) More emphasis should be given to those problems of pure mathematics which lie on the border between pure mathematics and applied fields — yet which aren't already exactly problems of applied mathematics,

(II) The tradition of earlier ICM's of giving talks in which the subject is not a mathematical theory but a real problem, and where the speaker in outlines shows how he or she has solved this problem by using mathematical methods, should be taken up again.

(III) Lectures (or perhaps whole sections or supplementary workshops) on the general prospects of various related fields of mathematics applications, providing the necessary background for a more profound debate about the relevance and the characteristic features of mathematical methods in that field, were recommended.

4. It was stated, by some of the participants, that the process of detente and the battle against racism and neocolonialism might be stimulated, if speakers invited to the ICM's adequately reflected the relative contributions of the various mathematical communities.

5. It was recommended that *national or regional communities of mathematicians* should be invited to give presentations at forthcoming ICM's, about the development of the mathematical life in their respective countries.

The project of an international publication, as a newsletter and a forum for debate.

This project appeared to be the main practical outcome that was proposed. Many questions were, however, raised about *the need, the content, the technical side and the realizability* of such a "journal".

1. Two main arguments were given for the project: firstly, such a publication as proposed in the working paper by Booss, was seen by some participants as a medium for an exchange of views between concerned people communicating their concerns, and as a step towards the possibility of formulating a policy which could serve as a base for further initiatives. Moreover, a need for a relevant and interesting "Mathematics Users Digest" with ready made information, which could bring different mathematical and mathematics-using circles closer together, was mentioned.

It was generally agreed that there exist several journals which would accept and which actually already publish articles of the kind desired at the conference. So, it was recommended to publish certain articles in different outlets, which are attainable at present. However, in the view of several participants this was not a good solution, because of the resulting diffusion of contributions. It was thought to be important to have a publication that would allow an exchange of experiences and ideas in a systematic way, rather than getting them lost in journals of different countries and different scientific milieux. In accumulating and putting together the various ideas, they will appear more clear, and the character and structure of the underlying concepts might come through.

2. Several proposals were made with respect to the *content* of such a publication. All of them seemed to fit well in the scheme (proposed in the working paper by Booss) of: *presentation of problems, ready-made short introductions, and a debate section.*

As to the possible ways of presenting some of the information desired, the following suggestions were made:

— In each issue a list and/or abstracts or digests of articles of interest to the readers of this "journal", which were published elsewhere, could be included,

— Excellent articles, taken from quite a wide range of topics, might be selected in some sort of "yearbook". This might be coordinated with the prize competition mentioned below, if it were established,

— Original contributions to the "journal" should mainly be short communications. Some participants wished reports on major conferences and other events of interest, in the different fields of application and pure research. Similarly it was suggested publishing series of reports about the mathematical life in different countries and in individual institutions of special interest.

3. There were no common conclusions on the intended *form of organisation* of such a publication. Some participants found that the International Mathematical Union (IMU) would be the appropriate organisation to run a publication with such broad aims. In contrast to this, other participants suggested starting in the simplest possible way with small ambitions and only a minimum of organisational needs. Along the latter line several suggestions were given:

— In the beginning it might be wise not to aim at publishing such a "journal" regularly, but rather on an intermittent basis.

— The editorial work should be initiated by a local (Danish) group of people, perhaps supplemented by correspondents from various countries and/or fields of specialisation, not necessarily writing contributors, but rather "observers" of scientific and "near"-scientific journals published within their respective areas of information, who could send copies of relevant materials to the Danish editors,

— Considerable attention should be paid to the way in which publication would be distributed. In view of the amount of office work that would be entailed, it was suggested seeking a financial system which would allow free publication for, say, the first two years, and then see what happens,

— It was estimated that if all relevant libraries should receive it, the minimum number of copies would be about one thousand,

— An animated debate arose concerning the problem of the language of the articles. No easy solution could be found to the dilemma that, on the one hand, mathematics as a part of any national culture, in a wide sense, should be communicated in the respective languages, and that, on the other hand, mathematics as a part of the joint scientific effort of mankind is dependent on easy international communication, which requires only one or a few languages of communication.

— A careful delimitation of the proposed new publication from existing journals would be necessary.

The proposal of organising further conferences.

It was recommended to organise further conferences in *continuation of the Roskilde Work-shop,* to deal in more detail with particular aspects of the problems touched upon. Such further conferences might allow more systematic investigations and more definitive con-tributions than were possible when dealing with the complex of problems in its totality!

The proposal of a prize competition.

A prize competition was proposed in order to stimulate the selection and generation of articles of the desired kind. The prize could be given for contributions within a wide range of topics, e.g. survey articles, conceptually new, or practical important applications, etc. Perhaps funds could be raised from industry. As one condition for receiving the prize, authors resp. publishers should agree to free reprinting of the awarded articles all over the world. A sponsorship by the IMU would be welcomed.

Initiatives to be undertaken on a local or national scale.

In accordance with the character of the workshop, the initiation of activities on an inter-national level was a central theme in the debate. The participants agreed however, that ini-tiatives which can and should be undertaken on a local or national scale in order to change the climate within and outside mathematical circles, are maybe the most essential ones:

— How to develop mathematical activity as a socially involved part of the programme for understanding and controlling nature?

— How to defend mathematics against antiscientific offensives? And how to develop the social responsibility of mathematicians and the true humanistic vigour of mathematics?

These questions, raised in the preceding discussions, cannot be answered purely on internal mathematical grounds. They need both considerations and actions in a total social context — and they need the participation of large numbers of interested people and not only of small minorities. From this it was argued that in the last instance international initiatives can play only a subsidiary role to the decisive steps which have to be undertaken on a local or national scale.

5. Working Papers

Ubiratan D'Ambrosio

Mathematics and the Developing Countries: Some Basic Issues

This paper will discuss the relationship between mathematics and the socio-cultural context in which it is placed. We will discuss some basic issues arising when trying to build up a mathematical research establishment in close relation with national priorities and goals. This brings into the discussion some questions which everyone working in closing the gap between the haves and the have-nots, which is at the root of our concern, has to face. These questions may be summarized as:

1. Is it possible to identify directions of mathematical research related to national priorities and goals?
2. If so, is it possible to conduct the training of mathematicians in the identified directions?
3. Is there the danger that the speed with which new problems and new

needs appear will not allow for the adequate preparation or adaptation of mathematicians, trained according to identified priorities and immediate needs, to cope with these new problems and needs?

It seems that these 3 questions summarize much of what individuals in charge of science policy must face, and to a great extent they represent a commonly identified anguish among some young mathematicians in developing countries. It has been long recognized that development generates needs never hitherto felt, and this is particularly true in scientific and technological development. On the other hand, the level of sophistication needed for scientific and technological advancement which are meaningful for priorities of development requires mathematical training which usually does not coincide with the most fashionable lines of research being produced in more developed countries. To some mathematicians in developing countries this is more appealing and a more immediate reward than facing the mathematical problems resulting from the national priorities which, although challenging, are sometimes unrelated to those in the top line of research in developed countries. This distortion, which sometimes meets the general backing of the cultural establishment, which to a certain extent shares these errors, can show some extremes, which reflects in a branching process which paradoxically opens the gap between mathematics, and in general the brain power of a country, and effective national priorities and needs. Although this is not less true in the developed world, in developing countries it has a sense of dramatic urgency, since these countries have to decide about the allocation of badly needed human and financial resources to a growing mathematical establishment.

Assuming that the three questions listed above have positive answers, and we have indications that this is the case just by looking into the way highly developed countries finance their research establishment, we need some strategies which may create a background and pilot ground for a deeper insight into those basic issues.

The strategy will require the following three major steps in the building up of a mathematical establishment in close relation with reality:

1. Identification of mathematical priorities, in an interdisciplinarian context and in deep relation to national developmental goals;
2. planning and implementing the preparation of human resources and facilities to carry on mathematical research leading to identified directions,

and at the same time organizing the productive sectors of the country to bring into the scene resulting problematics;

3. to build up mechanisms to keep the growing mathematical establishment in permanent renewal for fast absorption of recent mathematical advances which may contribute to newly identified developmental problems.

In dealing with strategies we insist on generating interdisciplinarian contexts, in which the various scientific disciplines are brought into play. The peculiarity of our situation calls for a high level of creativity in the application of existing science to unknown problematics. Scientific, in particular mathematical creativity in full relationship with the cultural environment in which this creativity takes place and finds its meaningfulness, can hardly be achieved in a fragmented disciplinary framework.

Bernhelm Booss

Some Ideas on the Launching of a Debate Journal on "Mathematics and the Real World"[+]

Motto: "Unite all mathematical efforts towards a better understanding and governing of our world!" (freely quoted from Fréchet)

Scope: Bring the different mathematical milieux together. Stress the interdisciplinary character of mathematics. Organize the contact between socially divided but theoretically interrelated activities. Collect and exchange and transfer "experience".

Address: People teaching mathematics, using mathematics, or producing mathematics with some sense for practical purposes.

Style: Entertainment, rapid orientation.

Production, Distribution, Calculation: Instead of producing the entire journal in one place, one might have matrices produced and mailed to certain distribution centers. This might diminish the cost of mailing and also would make the publication more dynamic. A non profit calculation could be based on 1 $ per issue, every issue with 64 pages, and 4 issues per year. The main edition should be in English. Satellite editions should probably be multilingual.

Contents: The profile, the shape, and the lay-out should be highly standardized. (This could facilitate the editorial work and shorten the deadlines for publication). I would suggest the following three sections: (1) In the "main section" (ca. 30 pages) correspondents of the journal would present "real" problems of practical and/or theoretical interest. Such "real" problems could consist of the successful prognosis of the water temperature in a river. Deep problems from theoretical mathematics, as f.ex. an announcement of new "practical" results in the field of spectral synthesis, should also be permitted. No presentation should exceed the limit of 2 (two) pages. 50% of that should consist of photographs or other material easy to visualize. The problems might already be solved or still under work. High priority should be given by the correspondents to stress conceptual new ideas either in the mathematical apparatus, or in the field of application, or in more general methodological aspects.

(2) A smaller section (of about 15 pages) should be devoted to present one region of the mathematical "folklore" to the general public in every issue. That could be "What *every* mathematicain should know on optimisation", or " ... on pattern recognition", or "... on 3-dimensional manifolds", or ... These articles should restrict themselves to the standard knowledge in that field, i.e. to those pieces of the "working language" usually concealed somewhere between the elementary not sufficiently advanced textbooks, and the prestigious research reports. They should be written in the tradition of the great encyclopedian articles, but — of course — more recent and thus more practical.

(3) In the last section (of some 15 more pages), the "debate" idea is to be considered in its true sense, i.e. in the form of a "written panel" section. This should be the place for a free discussion of highly controversial topics such

as the strategies of some publication houses or text book series, perspectives in the employment situation, experiences with continued mathematical education for "practitioners", criticism of and suggestions for the mathematical mass education, philosophical and ethical considerations, etc.

+ *Acknowledgements:* The project was already discussed (and, after the discussions, reshaped) with professors U. D'Ambrosio, Campinas; L. Collatz, Hamburg; B.V. Gnedenko, Moscow; J.P. Kahane, Paris; Ph. G. Kirmser, Kansas State Univ.; H. Matzke, Weimar; R. Selten, Bielefeld; L.D. Spraggs, Montreal.

Jelto Buurman, Ulrich Knauer

Some Aspects of the Relationship between Mathematics and Reality

In former times there seemed to be various philosophical, ideological, and economic reasons which prevented scientists, and mathematicians among them, from doing or publishing research. For example, for some time ideological reasons prevented the development of rationals, of complex numbers, of non Euclidian Geometries, and of Relativity Theory. On the other hand, ideological constraints often had a strong connection to reality in the sense that certain mathematical thoughts which did not seem to correspond with the given understanding of reality were not accepted. The disposing of such constraints, which of course is to be considered as progress, may be one reason for a weakening of the contact to reality. It might even provoke the view that a lack of connection from mathematics to reality is an advantage. Today in highly developed countries there doesn't seem to exist any philosophical or ideological constraints on the use of mathematical techniques. One exception possibly follows from a strictly intuitionist mathematical concept which, however, is not very influential. The attitude towards the directions of research activities, however, does not appear to be as free from constraints. As for mathematics, there is far too little impetus on research detecting further fields of applicability of mathematics. We claim that mathematics is to be used consciously to gain knowledge about reality and to dominate nature. In newer scientific essays like those of Heitsch[1], Ruzavin[2], Molodschi[3] and others, the problem of the relationship between mathematics and reality has been attacked theoretically.

(1) "The subject of mathematics is reality as a discrete and continuously structured, infinite variety of different objects." [4]

Consider the elements of a complicated system in the real world. The single causes for the phenomena are so various, that it is impossible to recognize them all at once; this means that the elements seem to us to be random. "It is interesting, that within the scope of logical, mathematical concepts it is possible to draw conclusions on certain relations of the elements in total abstraction from the underlying basic interconnections."[5] The central limit theorem is a fascinating example which shows that in a general way mathematical theorems and statements have an empirical content. On the other hand, theorems of this type are the foundations for technical algorithms which are applied to practical problems.

(2) Thesis: Just as technical and natural science are two components of a uniform process of perception and control of nature, there exist in mathematics two analogous components of the process of perception. The mathematical theorems and statements reflect reality – in a very general way – and the mathematical algorithms are general tools to change and control nature.

But the applicability of mathematics is viewed differently by different individuals. Are there any differences in research and results of different mathematicians dependent on their different views? One essential difference seems to consist in the direction and degree of relating results to problems of society.

Is there evidence that problems of various societies influence the development of mathematics? Certainly, highly developed countries can afford to have mathematicians work in any possible direction, which is presumably what is to be done. So far there has been no wrong or superfluous mathematics. But sometimes there has not been enough mathematics to solve various problems.

Possibly even the surprising events that, occasionally, pure mathematics all of a sudden becomes applicable are not just by chance, since mathematics reflects general tendencies of development in reality, as expressed by Riemann: "According to the concepts by which we perceive nature we do not only improve perception at any specific point but also certain future perception becomes determined as a necessary consequence."6)

It would probably be very useful to trace back which pure mathematical fields became important for application after they had been developed inside mathematics. Why and how did this happen and who promoted the process?

Comparing mathematics with natural sciences, another question arises. Is mathematics a quantitative science only or is it also qualitative? At least our example, the central limit theorem, is a qualitative statement. If we define quality as the system of important properties of an object, we have to conclude that the concept of quality is nearly the same as the concept of structure." Essential for a system are not only various connections. Speaking of a system implies to concentrate on the set of relations of its elements (here properties) and this is structure."7) But if we regard the process of perception, we see the following: When we consider an unknown object we first notice the phenomenal properties of this object and afterwards we quantify them in order to make them usable for us. Moreover, we notice that the process of developing a mathematical subject in depth is accompanied by a tendential algebraization. Less elaborated theories, that is, theories which so far developed in width, for example graph theory and even stochastic theories, are formulated to a smaller extent by algebraic means.

(3) Thesis: After the ancient greek scientists (Pythagoras, Euclid) restricted mathematics to the study of finite objects and geometry, mathematics has been viewed as a quantitative science. Since the last century the fields of application of mathematics were extended and with formalization and a strong development of structure theories and a tendential algebraization the old restriction was abolished.

Is there a tendential "probabilization" (stochastification) within mathematics today? If so, this is certainly influenced by the applications of mathematics. Research on the professional practice of mathematicians proves that stochastic theories are a general tool which all mathematicians working on practical problems need. Now we want to draw some "practical" conclusions from these theoretical considerations.

(4) Thesis: Because of the continuous growth of information of reality, specialization is a necessary process. Does this also imply a division between pure and applied mathematics?

(5) Thesis: To maintain an overall view, a specialist needs the following qualifications:

— wide and basic knowledge of mathematics
— knowledge of how mathematical theories are applied
— sociological and philosophical qualifications to an extent which enables the specialist to interpret his work in the social process.

(6) Thesis: Most of our textbooks do not reflect the process of discovery and development of mathematics which, of course, is a dialectical process. What they do is present the final results of long developments mostly in a completely ahistoric way, which, by the way, may also be a consequence of the liberation from ideological constraints.

(7) Thesis: To popularize theoretical results and impacts of application, popular scientific publications on a high but understandable level are needed. They can help scientists and practical workers to receive current information which may even lead them in a particular case to scientific work. This concept must contain a discussion of the sociological and philosophical implications mentioned above.

1. Heitsch, Wolfram, Mathematik und Weitanschauung, Berlin 1977
2. Ruzavin, G.I., Die Natur der mathematischen Erkenntnis, Berlin 1977
3. Molodschi, W.N.,Philosophische Probleme der Mathematik, Berlin 1977
4. Heitsch, S. 34: "Die Mathematik hat die Wirklichkeit als diskret und kontinuierlich strukturierte unendliche Manningfaltigkeit voneinander unterschiedlicher Dinge zum Gegenstand"
5. Leiser, Eckart, Einführung in die statistischen Methoden der Erkenntnisgewinnung, Köln 78, S. 233: "Interessant daran ist, dass es im Rahmen logisch, mathematischer Konzepte möglich ist, bestimmte Oberflächenzusammenhänge unter völliger Abstraktion von den ihnen zugrundeliegenden Vermittlungsgliedern abzuleiten."
6. by Molodschi, S. 107: "Nach den Begriffen, durch welche wir die Natur auffassen, werden nicht bloss in jedem Augenblick die Wahrnehmungen ergänzt, sondern auch künftige Wahrnehmungen als notwendig ... vorher ... bestimmt."
7. Thiel, Rainer, Mathematik, Sprache, Dialektik, Berlin 75, S. 55: "Denn wesentlich an einem System ist nicht nur, dass da etwas miteinander zusammenhängt. Von einem System

zu sprechen verpflichtet ja gerade, die Aufmerksamkeit auf die Menge der Beziehungen der Elemente (hier Eigenschaften) zu konzentrieren, also auf Struktur."

J. Casti

Mathematical Trends in System-Theoretic Research

According to von Neumann, "The origin of mathematics is in empirics". Evidence to support this claim is provided by the explosive developments of the past decade or so in mathematical system theory. Originally motivated by problems in electrical circuit theory, new mathematical concepts centering upon notions of feedback control, communication, stability and decision-making under uncertainty have been introduced. Fortunately, much of the *mathematical* foundations for these developments had already been laid by earlier work in linear algebra, matrix theory and differential equations, but the particular questions relevant to system-theoretic problems resulted in re-examination of this work and in substantial extentions and generalizations. We note the Kalman filter of optimal estimation theory as a particular example, as it represents a major theoretical and computational extension of Gauss' work on least-squares approximations. Other cases include Popov's extension of Lyapunov's stability result to cover certain nonlinear problems, the simplex method of linear programming, Zadeh's work on fuzzy sets and Bellman's Principle of Optimality in dynamic programming.

The question to now be addressed is whether such a trend of new mathematical developments can be expected to continue, or has the motivating influence of system problems run its course? Happily, all indications point to a continuation of past developments, although at a somewhat more sophisticated mathematical level. Most of the theoretical advances of the past few years have been in the area of *linear* mathematics, since the principal system-theoretic paradigm has been classical mechanics and the associated quadratic variational principles. Thus, the extensive developments in linear algebra, functional analysis, matrix theory and differential equations generated by system-theoretic questions were not totally unexpected. However, the pressure of a nonlinear world is now forcing theorists to break away from the above areas and to seek more powerful mathematical tools to break through the barrier of nonlinearity. Fortunately, past work in topology and algebra seems to be providing the key for such investigations.

In one direction, 19th and early 20th century work by Lie, Levi-Civitta, Chow and others on the interplay between differential equations and geometry is providing a substantial basis for deep results on controllability, observability and realization theory for broad classes of nonlinear processes. From a more combinatorial point of view, major advances in finite semigroup theory by Krohn, Rhodes, Eilenberg, et al. have provided important insights into both algebra and finite-state machines. Even more recently, work by Atkin based on combinatorial topology, has been fruitfully employed to study a variety of situations in the social and urban areas. As another case in point, the recent work on catastrophe theory is well-documented.

The key point to observe about all of the above-mentioned work is the way in which past ideas in "pure" mathematics have been resurrected, extended and modified by their employment in applied systems areas. The unavoidable conclusion is that the stimulus of even more realistic system-theoretic situations involving closer approximations to reality will most surely result in both extensive utilization of existing mathematical tools, as well as the transformations of classical pure mathematical ideas into new branches of applied mathematics.

Pierre Crépel

Compte-Rendu d'une Dissusion sur "Les Mathématiques et le Monde Réel"
tenue à l'Ecole d'Eté de Probabilités de Saint-Flour (France) le 10 juillet
1978.

Introduction

Les participants étant presque exclusivement des professionnels des mathématiques, essentiellement des enseignants-chercheurs, la discussion a été nette-
ment marquée par ce fait.

La plupart d'entre eux ont hésité à s'exprimer; pour beaucoup la raison prin-
cipale est que la forme choisie pour la discussion n'était pas la meilleure: en
petits groupes informels, au café, les gens parlent plus). Certains ont estimé
que cette réticence à s'exprimer était révélatrice d'un certain malaise, malaise
quelquefois inconscient :sentiment d'inutilité sociale, déception dans le choix
de profession, sentiment d'être le jouet de forces ocultes, peu de communication avec le monde extérieur, la production, la société.

Certaines des remarques faites dans la suite ont un caractère plutôt général
dans l'université, d'autres sont plus spécifiques aux mathématiques.

1. Les mathématiques sont-elles un jeu ou un outil issu de la pratique?

A l'échelle historique, les grandes théories mathématiques étaient toujours
venues de besoins de l'instant: autrefois les mathématiciens en étaient con-
scients car ils étaient très pluridisciplinaires (ex: apparition de la géométrie,
du calcul infinitésimal ...) Il semble qu'aujourd'hui encore les nouvelles théories (par exemple: nouveaux développements de la logique, linguistique mathématique) naissent de besoins pratiques précis (automatisation, électronique,
traduction automatique). Mais la grande masse des mathématiciens l'ignore ou
n'en est pas convaincue.

Dire cela n'épuise pas l'ensemble du problème.

D'autre part, le développement des mathématiques se fait aussi sans pression
de besoins externes: la création ne peut se faire que dans la liberté, on doit
admettre une certaine gratuité des actes; l'aspect jeu, plaisir personnel n'est

pas à rejeter et d'ailleurs permet le développemont de l'esprit créatif et l'amélioration de la connaissance mathématique et de la possibilité d'utilisation de l'outil mathématique.

Ces deux tendances sont-elles aussi inconciliables que cela peut paraître? Certains semblent penser que oui, et qu'il n'y pas à chercher des justifications sur l'utilité des mathématiques. D'autres pensent que lorsque le mathématicien, quelles que soient ses motivations, met au point un certain nombre de techniques ou établit des résultats, il serait souhaitable qu'il puisse s'intéresser à leur utilisation éventuelle, qu'un dialogue s'installe avec les utilisateurs potentiels. Ne serait-ce pas aussi une composante de sa liberté que de pouvoir maîtriser mieux l'ensemble du processus?

Cette question n'est pas étrangère à celle de savoir qui détient le pouvoir, comment sont prises les décisions concernant l'orientation des travaux mathématiques et leur utilisation.

2. Enseignement des mathématiques

–Les mathématiques jouent-elles actuellement le rôle d'accélérateur de la sélection (en particulier sociale)?

Pourquoi l'échec en mathématiques barre-t-il l'accès à des carrières même très éloignées des mathématiques? Les mathématiques sont-elles un outil de sélection mieux adapté que le latin, pourquoi?

Le caractère sélectif des mathématiques dans l'enseignement est-il dû à des propriétés intrinsèques des mathématiques ou aux conditions dans lesquelles se sont opérées les réformes de l'enseignement? Des avis partagés sont apparus dans la discussion.

Parmi les éléments de réponse possibles à cette question, citons: les carences dans la formation des maîtres, le manque d'information des parents (en particulier ceux des milieux sociaux les plus défavorisés), l'inadaptation des programmes (en particulier pour les sections et classes autres que terminale C) ... les élèves doivent apprendre des techniques sans savoir d'où elles viennent, ni qu'en faire, les facultés d'imagination, le côté "jeu", ne sont pas stimulés: les mathématiques sont vécues comme "em ... tes", la coordination entre les différents enseignements est faible.

—Les enseignants du secondaire qui sont intervenus se sont dits doublement déçus parce qu'ils n'ont pas les moyens d'assurer la mission qu'ils souhaitent et se sentent coupés de toute création mathématique.

Leur formation et les conditions de leur travail ne leur permettent guère d'échapper à cette réalité qui consiste à enseigner les choses de manière dogmatique.

—Les problèmes que soulève l'enseignement des mathématiques avant le baccalauréat ne sont pas seulement inhérents à la matière enseignée, mais dépendent d'un grand nombre de facteurs exterieurs (sociaux, économiques ...) sur lesquels la discussion ne s'est pas appesantie.

Ils sont également liés à la manière dont sont conçus les modes de diffusion des connaissances entre l'enseignement supérieur et la population (par exemple à travers la formation des maîtres ...).

3. Le(s) métier(s) de mathématicien

—Ce qui a été le plus ressenti dans la discussion, c'est que les préoccupations des mathématiciens sont davantage dirigées vers la ''recherche'' que vers les utilisations éventuelles ou même l'enseignement.

Ceci est à relier au fait que le cloisonnement des filières empêche les gens de maîtriser le processus, et à la coupure entre l'Université et le monde extérieur. Quelqu'un a remarqué que la politique d'intérêt à court terme des industriels français en est un élément de responsabilité important.

—Qu'est-ce qui motive les mathématiciens?

Chacun, bien sûr, a des motivations liées à son histoire personnelle, mais peut-on dégager quelques idées générales?

Pour la plupart, étant ''bons en mathématiques'' dans le secondaire, ils ont suivi la filière naturelle qui s'ouvrait devant eux, sans vocation véritable (même si nombre d'entre eux y trouvaient un certain plaisir).

La promotion sociale attachée aux fonctions de mathématicien ne semble pas avoir été un élément déterminant dans ce choix (peut-être est-ce discutable?). Alors se développe souvent un certain goût pour les mathématiques (connaissance, création, diffusion? ...) mais intervient une part de routine, d'obligation professionelle, et si ce goût s'estompe on se retrouve dans une impasse due en particulier au cloisonnement.

−Comment s'exerce le métier?

Dans l'enseignement supérieur, plusieurs tâches sont à remplir: tâches pédagogiques, recherche, formation continue, encadrement, tâches administratives diverses, contacts avec le monde extérieur, épistémologie, histoire des sciences ..., seuls l'enseignement et la recherche sont officiels, seule la recherche sert de critère pour la promotion interne. Cet état de faits engendre une tendance "productiviste" parfois nuisible à un fonctionnement plus sain.

Il est connu qu'un certain malaise est souvent dû à une insuffisance de l'encadrement, dont le rôle est pourtant reconnu fondamental. Mais le malaise a des origines plus larges (sociales, idéologiques ...) : par exemple, bien que la recherche procède largement par méthodes expérimentales, la manière dogmatique dont elle est diffusée masque cette réalité et contribue à un certain écoeurement ou à une sensation d'impuissance; d'autre part, la "communauté mathématique" (le terme serait à discuter) n'est pas étrangère aux différents conflits qui traversent la société. Il est net que tous les participants n'avaient pas la même analyse des causes et du caractère irréductible ou non de ces conflits.

Le déroulement des carrières (ou de carrières) ne satisfait visiblement personne: blocages, vieillissement, absence de débouchés pour les jeunes; la non-reconnaissance de la multiplicité des tâches accroît la rigidité du système. Sur les critères de jugement, l'opposition visible des avis (exprimés ou non) et la réticence à aborder le sujet de front n'ont pas dégagé d'idées directrices claires; seul constat: la diversité des aptitudes devrait interdire des expressions telles que "mathématicien de seconde zone".

Sur de problème des carrières, il y a aussi des avis différents, par exemple sur la mobilité des personnels et sur les conditions pratiques d'une telle mobilité.

Conclusion

A ce stade de la discussion, il est apparu que deux questions devaient être creusées en priorité
  — quel avenir pour les mathématiques et les mathématiciens?
  — quelles propositions pratiques peut-on envisager dans l'esprit de ce qui précède?

N.B. Ce compte-rendu a été rédigé par Pierre Crépel, Alain Huard et Daniel Prévot.

George F.D. Duff

**The Art of Teaching the Business of Modelling
in Applied Mathematical Science**

Mathematics is primarily an art because of its intellectual, creative, disciplined yet spontaneous and self-motivated character. The teaching of mathematics must, at the highest level, combine such diverse elements of structure and psychology that it, too, deserves to be regarded as an art.

The application of mathematics to many problems also embodies many characteristics of an art, but applied mathematics is governed by numerous internal laws and external constraints which may often limit severely the scope of intellectual creativity. Especially when large scale computation is involved, the use of mathematics in applied or engineering problems may be subject to limits of time and money that require it to be efficient. Thereby much of the modern work on the modelling of systems must partially take on the aspect of a business, both technically and administratively through research grant funding. In such endeavours a satisfactory yield of information or other results is expected in return for a given investment. A central problem for the teaching of applied mathematics in its modern model building aspect, therefore, is the reconciliation of art with business economy. Either one, alone, may be ineffective, but blended skilfully together they may succeed. Thus the modeller should be capable, so to speak, of wearing two different hats, putting on the one or the other as occasion demands, and also as we shall see, of wearing a suit of clothes compatible with both.

Models of physical systems are naturally subject to basic physical laws. For the fine points of sensitive interactive systems, delicate judgement will be required as to which effects or special laws can be safely ignored, and which combinations must be modelled in detail. Here the investigator must be alert, willing to follow the results of his own calculations even when they do not conform to his intuition, as well as having to check and recheck these results by all independent methods possible. That is, he and his models must be correctly clothed according to physical, natural and logical laws.

Thus the applied mathematician who models realistic systems must practise many diverse disciplines and skills, of which mathematics itself, though primary, forms only one part. He will often work as one member of a team containing diverse talents, so his skill in communication will be tested. Notwithstanding such collaboration, he will still need to sharpen his comprehension and critical judgement over a wide domain of problems, techniques and approaches.

That the civilized world has need of much modelling talent is evident on every hand, while many scientific, professional, and governmental organizations already exist devoted to the pursuit and encouragement of such work. The problem of teaching these skills to the oncoming generation is thus typical of situations in a highly developed complex system. Many specific avenues of improvement can be found, and most should be pursued.

The generation reaching maturity in the sixties and seventies has one great advantage over its predecessors, to wit a systematic training in means of using the modern computer. But the blending of effective large scale computation into models is now reaching the limits of diminishing return in many directions. A new round of sophisticated systemic, social, cybernetic and scientific concepts, such as resilience, pattern search, or entropy, are appearing as possible tools for the simulation of complex systems, and a future rapid evolution of concepts and techniques can be anticipated.

For the teacher and the educational writer, this extraordinary momentum must elicit the highest degree of technical breadth and expository skill, to outline the sustained evolutionary sweep of modelling technology, both hard and soft, to describe it in the round and to diagnose its strengths and limitations. A significant instance of a case history, for example, might be the global models developed for the Club of Rome, and the critical analyses that these have stimulated.

In almost every educational system, the perspectives and horizons of succeeding generations of teachers are limiting factors in the flexibility of the whole system. The system of higher education in mathematics and the natural and social sciences should find in itself the adaptability to educate talented undergraduate students in the many new dimensions of the modern trade of modelling in applied mathematics. The hardest part of such an adaptation is the laying aside of favourite theories and approaches and their replacement by less well tried topics and more recent techniques. But these steps must be taken, if the younger generation is to be reached at a formative age. We can then be confident that the oncoming generation will carry the development of applying mathematics to a still further evolutionary stage.

Should such a perspective seem too ambitious, we can remember that mathematics itself has taken in this century giant strides of structural generalization. Consider for instance the evolution from the theory of equations to the theory of categories. Whole theories became elements in wider structures, new analogies appeared, and existing methods were subsumed as special cases of new techniques. The teaching of applications of mathematics should reflect this wider and more powerfuld repertory, as well as the potentialities of the computer and the wider range of topics, problems and systems now accessible to quantitative study. The formidable challenge to teachers of applied mathematics is so to present the new powers and wider dimensions of their craft, that a comparable growth can be achieved in its systematic application.

Herman Duparc

Educational Aspects of Pure and Applied Mathematics

The role of mathematics in our present world differs essentially from the situation about half a century ago. Contrary to then there is hardly a problem where in some way mathematics and its related discipline informatics do not contribute either to a better understanding or to a better solution of our problems.

From this statement we have to draw our conclusions both on the educational and the research aspects of mathematics. We no longer believe that very specialised research is an every day affair in our mathematics curricula, it may even be doubted whether it should be a part of it at all.

The nature of mathematics induces two arguments to make the choice whether a chapter in mathematics should belong to such a curriculum or not:
  i. the use of such a chapter for further subjects which must be taught in the curriculum;
  ii. the use of that chapter in other disciplines or rather in some fields of life.

From this point of view the flow of mathematical knowledge may be divided in three parts:

  A. secondary school mathematics, to be taught to students between 12 and 18 years approximately;
  B. tertiary (university) mathematics, to be taught to students between 18 and 24 years approximately. This part of mathematics furnishes the major help in the applicational field.
  C. post-graduate mathematical studies, which might fill some people's complete further life. Here applications − if any − may help both in complicated and in some unexpected future fields of society.

Of course this division is valid for most educational activities, but here we want to emphasize the educational and applicational aspects of four flows in related developments:
  i. pure mathematics;
  ii. applied mathematics and informatics;

iii. disciplines which make use of mathematics and informatics;
iv. real world problems which ask for scientific help.

It is interesting to analyse the matrix M, the elements m_{ij} of which measure in some way the contributions of aspect i to aspect j (i,j run through the set 1,2, 3,4).

The element m_{12} indicates the inevitable and valuable help of pure mathematics to applied mathematics and informatics.

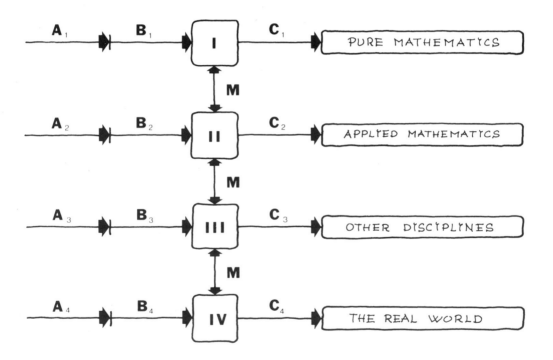

The element m_{21} deals with the influence of applications to pure mathematics. Nowadays this influence is important, it has been so in the past as well: from olden times to the present a good deal of mathematics has owed its development to this aspect.

The element m_{23} indicates the above mentioned important role of applied mathematics in other sciences, whereas m_{32} deals with the difficult problem of building the proper mathematical model for problems in those other sciences.

The element m_{34} measures the possibility of help from science to improve our world. In relation to m_{23} we see how mathematics contributes to this noble activity. The element m_{43} deals with the direct demands for scientific help in everyday problems of our world.

The elements m_{ij} with $|i-j| \geqslant 2$ indicate more vague relations; maybe statistics comes in the picture when studying m_{42}.

In the diagram below the interrelations M were placed at the end of phase B. With the help of the phase C knowledge a new relation matrix M at a higher level might be obtained.

One might further estimate the relative values of all elements m_{ij} in order to construct a good curriculum of pure and applied mathematics and informatics. It is not advisable to overemphasize one aspect or interrelation, this might spoil the balance. From this point of view a good university mathematics curriculum should contain most of the applicational aspects and only a limited number of theoretical aspects. A proposal in Holland, started in 1968, to split up university curricula into those two parts was unfortunately disapproved even by a good deal of university staff. We might hope that one arrives at a better conclusion in the next decade.

Geoffrey Howson

Mathematics and the Real World: Some Consequences for Teacher Training

"Anxious inquiry into ... mathematical problems leads away from the things of life, and estranges men from a perception of what conduces to the commen good"

Juan Luis Vives

"Mark all mathematical heads which be wholly and only bent on these sciences, how solitary they be themselves, how unfit to live with others, how unapt to serve the world"

Roger Ascham

"It is well ascertained fact ... that mathematicians ... do of all men show the least judgement for the practical purposes of life, and are the most helpless and awkward in common life"

Prince Albert

These comments by tutors to two English queens and by the husband of a third illustrate a view of mathematics and its practioners that has been commonly held for many centuries: a view which would not have persisted so long had it not contained an element of truth!

One purpose of our short seminar is to investigate the temptation to which Vives referred and how it might be overcome. In this paper my concern is how society's attitudes towards mathematics can be changed. I take it as "axiomatic" that in general a person's attitude to the subject is largely based on the mathematics teaching he receives. Consequently, the first step towards fostering a new appreciation of mathematics is to reappraise the education of future teachers (at all levels) and to see what view of mathematics it is designed to inculcate and what experience it provides of the subject and of its applications.

This idea is by no means novel and accounts can be found of attempts to design new courses for intending teachers (see, for example, [2], [4]). It is significant to warn, however, that these courses depend considerably on the staff of, and the opportunities offered within, particular institutions. They are largely "material-free" and as such will not be easily replicated elswhere. A feature of the two schemes to which I refer is the emphasis placed on modelling — a form of mathematical activity on which considerable attention is currently being focussed. Its importance and significance is not to be denied. Yet, if we are not to see yet another false dawn, it must be emphasised that innovators have a duty not only to develop courses within their own institutions, but also to spell out their philosophy and aims carefully and in detail, and to provide teaching materials, ideas and/or training for others. If this is not done, then the process of diffusion may be disastrous and the message will reach less gifted colleagues in a garbled, valueless form. In particular, it will be necessary to distinguish clearly between the aims of developing the ability to model, and to appreciate the art of modelling. We must also take care to determine whether our primary concern is to demonstrate how mathematics can be used to solve real problems, or to find "real-life- motivation" — often of a dubious nature — for teaching pure mathematics.

Perhaps one example will suffice to demonstrate that there is, indeed, a problem of teacher training. "Mathematics as a Second Language" [3] is a book written "for use in courses for liberal arts students and for prospective elementary school teachers". It sets out "to show how mathematics affects almost every aspect of our lives" and is remarkably succesful in attaining its aims: there are some well written chapters on applications of matrices, game theory, linear programming, probability and statistics. However, and here's the rub, the proposed two-semester course for prospective teachers omits these chapters. The teachers are offered a diet of sets, logic, number bases, the real number system, mathematical systems (groups), geometry and number theory. To adopt the authors' metaphor, it appears to suffice for teachers to know the grammar of mathematics, its literature need not concern them!

As mathematicians we glory (and perhaps take refuge) in the fact that unlike educationists, social scientists and others, we teach students *"to do"* and *not "to appreciate"*. Yet when one talks of the place of mathematics in society and even within the curriculum, one is forced back on appreciation rather than action. Such an appreciation will not come merely via a course on modelling, or even through the industrial experiece provided by some teacher-training institutions. A careful study of a few applications may also fail to provide a wide perspective: depth plus perspective would seem desirable. Yet how is this to be achieved? Some key questions to be considered would appear to be:

1. How can one design a course (or a textbook) leading to an "appreciation" of the role of mathematics in society? (Can one, in fact, "appreciate" mathematics without doing it: are the analogies of music and art inappropriate?) What level of mathematical knowledge is required to "appreciate" an application of mathematics? (Experience of history essays in which students are clearly ignorant of the mathematics whose significance they are discussing, makes me have some reservations.) Is "appreciation" the wrong word — does one

"appreciate" the clarity or subtlety of a proof, but "understand" an application? How does one assess a student's "appreciation"?

(The difficulties are formidable; yet, unless they are overcome, teachers are likely to continue to have an ill-balanced view of mathematics and problems of ill-designed curricula will remain.)

2. Is there a need to ensure that all student-teachers have some contact with creative mathematicians (either from industry or educational institutions) and an opportunity to learn of their motivation and methods?

3. If courses of the kind I describe plus, perhaps, industrial experience or simulations/case studies (see, for example, [1]) are included in teacher-training, what traditional components are we willing to omit in order to make room for them?

References
[1] Clements L.S. and Clements R.R., "The objectives and creation of a course of simulations/case studies for the teaching of engineering mathematics". *Int. J. Math. Educ. Sci. Technol.*
1978, $\underline{9}$(1), 97-117.

[2] Howson, A.G., "University courses for future teachers", *Educ. Stud. in Math,* $\underline{6}$, 1975, 273-292.

[3] Newmark, J. and Lake, F. *Mathematics as a second language,* Addison Wesley, 1975 (3rd printing).

[4] Niss M., "The 'crisis' in mathematics instruction and a new teacher education" *Int. J. Math. Educ. Sci. Technol.,* 1977, $\underline{8}$ (3), 303-321.

Mogens Esrom Larsen

Aspects of Complementarity in the Application of Mathematics

The use of the concept of complementarity requires two objects. In this context the first object is the reality, and the second one is our model. The question is how do these two objects interact?

I should like to consider the reality as a set of events furnished with some stochastic variables. These stochastic variables are what we can see. They must obey some simultaneous distribution which we do not know. Our model claims that a function from the stochastic variables into some space has some properties. More generally a model could be any statement about the distribution mentioned above.

The philosophy in physics is (or was) that the behavior of the variables is independent of the existence of our model. The complementarity came into physics with the remark that the variables are somehow dependent on whether we look at them or not.

If we want to consider the real world of human activities, it seems that other ways of model-dependence may appear. As the events are influenced by decisions, these events are influenced by consideration of the world which may be our model. In a predictive model we may choose our behaviour in relation to predictions. And in a descriptive model we can use the description to substitute for more elementary satisfaction.

As an example of the last possibility I should like to point to the concept of balance of payments. Some economic models lead the government to believe that we will be most happy exporting more than we import. As a consumer I should feel more happy in the opposite situation.

As an example of the first possibility I want to take the stock market. Let us suppose we offer a predictive model with the conclusion, that the rate of exchange is going to increase. If the model is accepted by stockholders, they should decide to buy more stocks, and prices are likely to increase. It seems not to matter what the substance of the model is. But further, we could exchange increase with decrease (and buy with sell). This means that even if we take the fixpoint aspect, claiming that a good predictive model must predict the behavior, which is going to happen when the model is known, we cannot choose the better model.

The conclusion is that any model of reality affects this in several ways and among those also such ways that make statistical tests absurd.

Rangaswami Narasimhan

Mathematics and the Study of Complex, Information-Processing Behaviour

1. Historically, many of the formal systems that have now become classical in mathematics have had their origins in the study of the physical world. The relationship between science (i.e., natural philosophy) and mathematics can be briefly outlined in these terms. Through controlled interactions with the environment a scientist is often able to delimit a certain class of events. He then tries to construct a formal theory of this class of events through suitable abstractions, simplifications and assumptions. When these abstractions, simplifications, and assumptions are formulated as axioms, there results a formal system suitable for study by mathematicians. They can then investigate what kinds of theorems such an axiom system gives rise to, the relationship between this axiom system and other axiom systems, and similar problems.

This manner of interaction between science and mathematics during the last two or three centuries has paid rich dividends when it has been applied to the study of physical systems. But attempts to extend this methodology to the study of biological systems have been far less successful. I think it is important to understand the reasons for this failure. The spectular accomplishments of the physical sciences in predicting and controlling physical events have led scientists trying to study biological/behavioural systems to assume that prediction and control are the essence of scientific activity, and quantification and measurement are the most important methodological tools.

However, the characteristic aspect of organismic behaviour consists in the fact that an organism has a repertoire of *actions* which it uses to interact with its environment and to manipulate it to satisfy its needs. It is this fact, that a biological organism is capable of functioning as an *agent* and not merely as an *object* wholly subservient to the manipulations of external agencies, that is of central concern to behavioural studies.

In trying to model the agentive aspect of agents, the behavioural sciences have to cope with three categories of explanations, in general. Firstly, there are the explanations that are concerned with the nature of any given action belonging to the action repertoire of an agent. A satisfactory explanation would, presumably, try to account for a given action in terms of a set of sub-actions suitably sequenced and related. Actions can only be accounted for in terms of information processing systems. For actions manipulate the external environment and, hence, call for the sensing and analyzing of the state of this environment, and require the deployment of appropriate control *actions* to arrive at the desired state of affairs. Information processing systems endowed with the appropriate sensors and effectors are designed precisely to accomplish such tasks.

The second class of explanations in the behavioural sciences would then be concerned with the physiological realizability of such information processing systems. Such explanations would concern themselves with the kinds of building blocks used and their interconnections, as well as with the properties of such building blocks and the developmental aspects of these physiological subsystems and systems.

The third class of explanations arises when one seeks to account for particular occurrences of actions or states of agents. This particular agent is at this moment doing this; it is in this state. At some specified previous time it was in another specific state and doing something else. Such specific events call for explanations: why these events at these moments and not others? A scientific theory, we normally assume, should be able to postulate a set of behavioural *laws* on the basis of which the occurrences of such specific events could be predicted or accounted for.

Even assuming that a science of behaviour is ultimately concerned with prediction and control, one cannot hope to cope with these without first coming to grips with the first two categories of explanations. Knowledge of the behavioural acts and of the mechanisms that underlie behaviour is a prerequisite to any attempt at control or shaping of behaviour.

2. Those familiar with the operation of digital computers are only too painfully aware of the limitations and inadequacies of currently available mathematical formalisms and techniques to deal with complex information processing systems that can interact with their environments and are capable of describing and manipulating them. Consider, for example, a time-sharing computing system that can service a large number of users interacting with it from terminals employing a variety of languages. There is, as yet, no general mathematical formalism available which would enable us to design such interactive information-processing systems systematically and efficiently. Digital computers of this kind are perhaps the most complex man-made information processing systems. Yet, even the simplest naturally occurring organism is vastly more complicated compared to the most complex digital computers in operation today. We do not have an appropriate mathematical formalism to characterize the dimensions of complexity of these naturally occurring organisms.

Studies that computer scientists have been carrying out during the last two decades or so in simulating the behaviour of man-made and naturally occurring information processing systems seem to show conclusively that computational approaches to modelling these systems are likely to be the most appropriate and viable. Notions like syntax, semantics and pragmatics of behaviour play an essential role in articulating these approaches. Naturally-occurring organisms seem to possess yet another mode of behaviour that finds no counterpart in the operation of digital computers at all. This is the perceptual (sensory-motor-level) mode of behaviour. Concepts like intuitive, informal, tacit, paradigmatic, etc., relate to this mode of behaviour. Our current understanding at the computational-level of this mode of behaviour is next to nothing.

3. I believe that the creation of formalisms and techniques to cope with the behaviour of complex information-processing systems — systems with sensory modalities and an action repertoire which can interact with their environments and manipulate them — is likely to pose the greatest challenge to mathematics and mathematicians of the future.

Tim Poston

Structure and Application

I query the assumption, in much of the "Catalogue of questions", that the gap between mathematics and its application is widening. At least as good a case could be made for the view that the "lead time" between a mathematical development and its application is shrinking steadily. The number $\sqrt{-1}$ was introduced for "pure" reasons centuries before a physics and electronics for which it was essential appeared; Hilbert's spectrum of an operator took decades to become the spectrum of an atom; while from Thom's conception (long predating proof) of his classification of the elementary catastrophes, to the first experimental confirmations of new physical and biological predictions from it, was less than ten years.

These examples are not wholly representative: the theory of "degrees of undecidability" currently looks as far from application as that of nowhere-differentiable curves (now central to diffusion theory) looked last century; but in either direction there is at least a case to answer.

Furthermore, the distaste for even the possibility of application current earlier this century (archetypified by G.H. Hardy) is losing ground. The positive hunger for application is illustrated by such incidents as an algebraic geometer, wholly "pure" in background, turning up at a biology department with a wish to apply catastrophe theory. Nothing resulted (it is not that easy – and some bad science has resulted from supposing it is), but the mathematical mood is back to marvelling at the real world. This conference is a symptom of a trend, not a voice crying in the wilderness.

The problem, then, is how to do *better* something that is being done – if not well – at least not impossibly badly: to bring mathematical developments into contact with potential applications. The development of "appropriate mathematics" does not require separate measures – contact once made, feedback will stimulate new mathematics (as planetary motion problems created calculus and topology).

Such contact requires a certain frame of mind, in both teaching and research. Suggestions for institutional or regulatory measures should be considered with care and caution, lest they prove as counter-productive as Nixon's "War on Cancer" at the expense of basic research. Indeed, the British institution of "Applied Mathematics Departments" is just such a mistake: in too many there is neither mathematics done of any conceptual integrity (let alone awareness of new developments in mathematics proper), nor real application to problems where experiment could answer back. (Cf. the Royal Society report "Postgraduate Training in the UK 4: Applied Mathematics"). Certainly, if trained in one I could not have become equipped to write a book ranging over naval architecture, fluid mechanics, scattering theory, buckling, lasers, ecology — and be told by a scientist to whose work one chapter is devoted that it taught him new things about his own subject. This resulted not from personal cleverness but from attitude; attention to the central mathematical vision, which a "pure" education taught me, followed by sustained contact with users of mathematics addressing scientific problems.

In a world looking more and more to organisational structure, both for description and prescription, it is perhaps unfashionable to preach the value of personal example. But I suggest that any proposed institutional fix should be measured rather against "Will it permit — not hinder — good teaching with awareness of the unity of mathematics and its applications?" than against delusory hopes that it might *produce* these good results. No scheme will produce them, just as no syllabus is usefully "reformed" when filtered through primary school teachers with high anxiety scores over their own elementary mathematics. But many of the students of a good teacher will communicate well themselves — if they are allowed to.

G.S. Ramaswamy

The Role of Mathematics in the Engineering Sciences:
Present Status and Future Possibilities

(1) Objects of the workshop

The workshop, as I see it, is expected to create an interface between the generators and users of mathematics so that the two groups can think together and identify:

i) Areas of mathematics which have already demonstrated their usefulness in the service of the sciences, and
ii) New areas with promising potentialities for applications in Science and Engineering in the foreseeable future.

Incidentally, the workshop may also serve the very useful purpose of bridging the chasm that often separates mathematicians pursuing their specialized areas of interest more or less in isolation.

Obviously, the first objective is very much easier to accomplish than the second. This does not mean that *all* engineers and mathematicians are fully aware of the areas of mathematics that are already being utilized in the service of the sciences. Only an elite group of mathematically trained engineers and mathematicians working in close association with engineers have explored these possibilities to some extent on an ad hoc basis. Even here, much remains to be done.

The second objective is certainly more ambitious and is in the nature of crystal-gazing but is certainly worth undertaking. These efforts to foresee future applications for specialized branches of mathematics are characterized by Stanislaw Ulam[1] as "patrols" sent out in all directions in the hope that some of them will produce useful results.

(2) Inhibiting Factors

The following inhibiting factors create a communication barrier between the community of applied scientists and engineers on the one hand and mathematicians on the other.

i) The mathematician is looking for "clean problems" to which he can readily apply the techniques he knows. Or in other words, the engineer or the scientist has to pick up the problem from the factory floor or the field, idealize it and offer it to the mathematician in a form that he can comprehend.
Practical problems will have to be shorn of confusing details before they can be reduced to mathematical form.

A parable will best illustrate this situation. A passer-by sees a drunk searching for something on a well-lit pavement.
"What are you looking for?" asks the passer-by.
"I am looking for a lost ten dollar bill," says the drunk.
"Did you lose it here?"
"No," says the drunk, "I lost it in the garbage heap."
"Don't you think that it is more logical to look for it there?" asks the passer-by.
"No," says the drunk, "The garbage heap is full of broken glass. It is easier to look for it here."

Practical problems are far from clean and clear and for this reason, one prefers the well-lit pavement to the garbage heap. The question is: Who will clean them up? This task can be undertaken only by a community of "go-betweens" who are either mathematically-trained engineers or mathematicians with sufficient knowledge of other sciences or engineering. Their tribe must increase.

ii) Even now, we have such "go-betweens", although their number tends to be small. But what often happens is that they become fascinated with the techniques and tools themselves and a situation soon develops when we have techniques in search of problems (reminding one of Lugi Pirondello's play "Charracters in Search of an Author").

iii) The "gem-finders" are few but the gem-polishers are many. The "gem-finders" are the trail-blazers who have the skill to idealize problems and find suitable mathematical tools and techniques to solve them. When once the trailer-blazers have done their job, others make a bee-line to that area and overwork it and make endless refinements instead of going into new uncharted areas which will be more worthy of their efforts. An example will best illustrate this situation.

For carrying out the stress analysis of complex engineering structures (including the human skeleton in bio-mechanics), engineers were obliged to develop mathematical models which are suitable for computerization. By a pragmatic process, the finite element technique for discretization of continua was developed for this purpose. This was something of a break-through and this versatile technique has found applications in solving problems in structural analysis, fluid mechanics, rock-mechanics and bio-mechanics during the past decade. The result has been that in the recent past almost every graduate thesis in the engineering sciences has been devoted to this technique.

(3) Suggestions for Breaking down the Communication Barrier

i) This workshop is a good beginning. It needs to be followed up by similar periodic workshops arranged for each area of microspecialization of engineering and science to provide meeting grounds for scientists, engineers and mathematicians.

ii) The content of mathematics taught to scientists and engineers needs to be continually up-dated. The mathematics taught to undergraduates in science and engineering has remained practically static and stagnant during the past twenty years. The task of up-dating needs to be entrusted to a "brainstrust" of the ablest mathematicians, engineers and scientists interested in the future of mathematics and its applications.

(4) Some Thoughts on the Future Role of Mathematics in
the Engineering Sciences

4.1 Possibly, I may start this survey by mentioning areas of mathematics which in my personal experience have already demonstrated their usefulness to engineers:

1) Laplace Transforms
2) Matrix Algebra
3) Stochastic Processes
4) Linear, non-Linear and Dynamic Programming
5) Optimazation Techniques
6) Discretization Techniques for Modelling Continua with infinite degrees of freedom by systems with a finite degree of freedom. The Finite Element Techniques are examples.
7) Numerical Methods of Integration
8) Solution of Boundary Value Problems by Integral Equations.
9) Markov Processes
10) Graph Theory

4.2 The scope for future applications of mathematics can to some extent be anticipated if forecasts can be made of the possible directions of growth of the engineering sciences. I will try to do this for Structural Engineering which is my discipline. Similar exercises need to be carried out for each scientific and Engineering discipline.

Shapes of Structures
In the past, it has been the practice in the design process to assume the shape of structures to start with, without reference to the material of which they are made. Or, in other words, the geometry and topology are arbitrarily chosen as the point of departure. A stress-analysis is then carried out. This unnatural process often leads to lengthy and tedious calculations. Sometimes ill-continued equations result, indicating an inappropriate choice of shape. There are many advantages to be gained in reversing this process. A desirable state of stress that the material will sustain can be selected. We may then ask for the appropriate shape of the structure to achieve this state of stress. An example will best illustrate this statement. Suppose the structure is to be built of concrete. It is known that concrete can carry high *compressive* but negligible *tensile* stresses. It is then logical to look for a structural form which will carry loads in pure compression. For example, I had demonstrated 2) that it can be done if the structural shape chosen is a funicular shell. In effect, we have reversed the normal sequence followed in design practice. *The stress has been chosen and the shape found.* It can be rigorously demonstrated that the resulting shape is optimal. In future, stress-analysis is likely to be supplanted by this process structural synthesis. The development of mathematical

tools and techniques needed for finding optimal shapes, given the loads and the properties of materials is an area that is likely to prove important.

Loads and Properties of Materials

The current practices relating to design of structures are based on a *deterministic philosophy*. So are the currently employed concepts of safety. The maximum loads that are likely to occur are given in the Codes of Practice. So are the allowable stresses. These have a deterministic format. There are some attempts at present to specify loads and stresses in a semi-probabilistic format but these are not thorough-going enough. Similarly, the calculations of responses of structures under loads — deflexions, stresses, etc. are also done on a deterministic basis. But the loads on structures are subject to variability. So are the material properties. In future, a *stochastic* approach is likely to replace this deterministic approach. This trend is also likely to be accentuated by the new materials that are around the corner — fibre reinforced composites, polymer concrete, etc. A few studies have already appeared using Monte Carlo methods to predict responses of structures. Systematic and coherent approaches to such problems are a practical necessity. The rheology of materials and means of incorporating them in design and the modelling of real materials are other challenges that structures of the future will present. The ageing of structures and the consequent changes in their responses are problems that await mathematical analysis. The analysis of structures right up to collapse after they have cracked also opens up new avenues for study.

(1)   Ulam, S., "The Application of Mathematics". In: "The Mathematical Sciences", a Collection of Essays edited by COSRIMS (Committee on Support of Research in the Mathematical Sciences), M.I.T. Press, 1968.
(2)   Ramaswamy, G.S., "The Theory of a New Funicular Shallow Shell of Double-Curvature", Indian Concrete Journal, September 1960.

Mohammad El Tom

On Future Mathematics in Underdeveloped Countries

I. The share of world trade in the hands of underdeveloped countries is about 20%. I suspect that the contribution of these countries to the mathematical literature is much smaller.[+]

With the exception of a few of the larger countries, graduate education in mathematics is extremely weak in this part of the world. Therefore, it is hardly meaningful to speak of dominant trends in the mathematical activity of the area. However, more indigenous Ph. D.'s are continuously flowing into these countries and important steps have or are being taken to strengthen graduate programs in mathematics. The time seems to be right to inquire about the characteristics of future (1990's and ownwards) mathematics in underdeveloped countries.

I want to briefly discuss a number of (external and internal) factors which I believe will play an important part in shaping future mathematics in a large number of underdeveloped countries.

II. External factors
The centre of mathematical activity lies in the industrialized nations; and mathematics being what it is, a universal science, third world mathematicians are bound to be influenced to a greater or lesser extent by what goes on in the centre.

1. This influence exerts itself primarily though training. Although I have no statistics, I would guess that about 70% of third world[++] Ph.D's in mathematics either received their doctorate degrees or did a post-doctoral training in U.S.A., U.K., or France. This situation is not likely to be qualitatively altered in the near future. Even if heretofore the majority of younger mathematicians receive all their training locally, the weight of the older and Western-trained mathematicians is not likely to be appreciably diminished in the near future.

   The effect of training is most visible in the similarity of structures of third world university mathematics institutions and corresponding ones in the West. These structures include forms of organization, courses of study, graduate education and systems of promotion and recognition.

2. An important and obvious source of influence are publications, conferences and organizations. In research and mathematics education, dominant trends and fashions in the centre are most likely to prevail elsewhere.

In the absence of other strong factors, the combined effect of these two and related secondary factors is to generate a mathematical activity which, while probably well-integrated in the mainstream of mathematics, has very little impact on third world societies[+++]. Mathematics will eventually stagnate. Fortunately, however, there are some other important factors, which are likely to greatly weaken this tendency.

III. Internal forces

The forces described below influence the development of all the sciences. However, it seems that their influence is greatest on mathematics.

1. Developing nations have long been convinced of the necessity of indigenous science to (material and cultural) development. A prerequisite for the establishment of a national science capability is the achievement of self-determination in science. The realization of this condition implies that local scientists must bear full responsibility for the development of their disciplines and it allows for critical assessment of achievements (or lack of them).

Once achieved, however, self-determination in science does not by itself necessarily lead to the attainment of the objective of indigenous science. Indeed, the relationship between the two concepts is in many ways similar to that between "national self-determination" and "development".

2. Perhaps, the source of the strongest influence on the activities of third world intellectuals is their awareness of the phenomenon of underdevelopment. Contrary to the widely-held belief that poor job opportunities and low salaries provide a satisfactory explanation of the observed "scarcity of talent" in mathematics, I believe that this "awareness of underdevelopment" often leads brilliant students to choose for their studies those disciplines which are seen by them to be *relevant* to

their societies. The implications of relevance on the orientation of mathematics are obviously considerable.

3. The difficulty and urgency of development on the one hand, and the
   scarcity of resources on the other hand, lead to the adoption of planning,
   at various levels, as a tool for accelerating development. An important
   instance of aspects of this activity is the Chinese National Science Conference held in March, 1978.

   Science policies usually put much greater emphasis on those areas of
   science which seem to be of importance to major developmental problems. The clarification and solution of these problems is unlikely to be
   appreciably advanced outside an interdisciplinary framework. Moreover,
   the production quality of scientists necessary for tackling these problems
   poses in turn enormous educational ones.

   The combined effect of these internal factors is to encourage team work,
   deemphasize pure mathematics and foster research in problems of mathematical education, interdisciplinary studies and in those areas whose
   range of applicability is relatively wide.

IV. Conclusion

Future mathematical activity in a large number of underdeveloped countries
will be partly shaped by the interplay of the external and internal factors
discussed above. Recent activities on national, regional and international
levels strongly indicate that the internal factors will dominate. Consequently,
I foresee the following as important characteristics of future mathematics in
these countries.
   a. A smaller proportion of mathematicians who are active in major areas
      of pure mathematics;
   b. The emergence of statistics, applied probability, operations research,
      computational mathematics, computer science and mathematical educat-
      ion as strong areas.
   c. The (relatively slower) emergence of interdisciplinary studies such as
      mathematical economics and biomathematics as active areas of research.
   d. A larger proportion of mathematicians involved in collaborative research
      effort.

All this, however, depends on the existence of sufficiently enlightened and stable political systems in these countries.

+   Of about 1500 journals listed in the Mathematical Review, about 8% are published in third world countries and of these 30% are Indian.

++   India is probably an exception.

+++   I view mathematics as a human social activity that interacts with the socio-cultural milieu in which it takes place.

Appendix 1. Bibliography

Else Høyrup:
Books *about* Mathematics: History, Philosophy, Society, Psychology,
Teaching, Models, Systems etc.

Contents:

History of mathematics, in general
History of mathematics, special
   epochs and cultures
History of mathematics, special
   topics
Philosophy of mathematics, in general

Philosophy of mathematics, special
   topics
Miscellanies about mathematics
Sociology of mathematics
Mathematics and society and politics
Psychology of mathematics
Mathematics teaching
History of mathematics teaching

An enlarged version of this bibliography can be acquired by writing to Else Høyrup, Roskilde University Library, P.O.Box 258, DK 4000 Roskilde, Denmark. Suggestions of further
titles will be welcomed.

Recreational mathematics
Untraditional mathematics books
Mathematization
Mathematical models
Systems, in general
Systems, special topics
Mathematics and women
Countries, past (from 1500) and present
   Africa
   Bulgaria
   Canada
   China
   England

   France
   FRG
   GDR
   Germany
   Italy
   Soviet Union
   USA
How to write mathematics
Bibliographies
Dictionaries
Handbooks
Encyclopedias
Addresses

History of Mathematics, in General

Ball, W.W. Rouse: A Short Account of the History of Mathematics.
1888. New York: Dover, 1960 (reprint).
Bourbaki, N: Eléments d'histoire des mathématiques.
Paris: Hermann, 1960, 1974.
Boyer, Carl: A History of Mathematics.
New York: Wiley, 1968.
Cantor, Moritz: Vorlesungen über Geschichte der Mathematik.
4 vols. Leipzig 1900-1908. New York: Johnson Reprint, 1965.
Eves, H: An Introduction to the History of Mathematics.
1953. New York: Holt, Rinehart and Winston, 1969.
Kline, Morris: Mathematical Thought from Ancient to Modern Times.
New York: Oxford University Press, 1972.
Sarton, George: The Study of the History of Mathematics and The Study of the

History of Science.
1936. New York: Dover, 1957 (reprint of two originally separate volumes).
Smith, David Eugene: History of Mathematics.
2 vols. 1923. New York: Dover, 1958.
Smith, David E. (ed.): A Source Book in Mathematics.
2 vols. New York, 1929. New York: Dover 1959.
Struik, Dirk J: A Concise History of Mathematics.
New York: Dover, 1948, 1967.
Struik, D.J: A Source Book in Mathematics, 1200-1800.
Cambridge, Massachusetts: Harvard University Press, 1969.

History of Mathematics, Special Epochs and Cultures

Biernatzki, K.L: Die Arithmetik der Chinesen.
Berlin, 1855. Wiesbaden: Martin Sändig Reprint, 1973.
Bochner, Salomon: The Role of Mathematics in the Rise of Science.
Princeton: Princeton University Press, 1966.
Datta, B. and Singh, A.N: History of Hindu Mathematics.
2 vols. Lahore, 1935-38. Bombay: Asia Publishing House, 1962 (reprint).
Dubbey, J.M: Development of Modern Mathematics.
London: Butterworths, 1970.
Gillings, Richard J: Mathematics in the Time of the Pharaohs.
Cambridge, Massachusetts: MIT Press, 1972, 1975.
Heath, T.L: A History of Greek Mathematics.
2 vols. Oxford: At the Clarendon Press, 1921.
Juschkewitsch, A.P: Geschichte der Mathematik im Mittelalter.
Leipzig: B.G. Teubner, 1964.
Juschkewitsch, A.P: Les mathématiques arabes (VIIIe-XVe siècles)
French translation. Paris: J. Vrin, 1976.
Kaye, G.R: Indian Mathematics.
Calcutta: Simla, 1915.
Klein, Felix: Vorlesungen über die Entwicklung der Mathematik im 19ten Jahrhundert.
2 vols. Berlin, 1926-27. New York: Chelsea, 1950.
Mikami, Yoshio: The Development of Mathematics in China and Japan.
Leipzig and Berlin, 1913. New York: Chelsea, 1961 (reprint).
Needham, Joseph: Science and Civilization in China. Vol. 3: Mathematics and the Sciences of the Heavens and the Earth.
London: Cambridge University Press, 1959.
Neugebauer, O: The Exact Sciences in Antiquity.
Princeton, 1952. New York: Dover, 1969.
Smith, David Eugene and Mikami, Yoshio: History of Japanese Mathematics.
Chicago: The Open Court, 1914.
Srinivasiengar, C.N: The History of Ancient Indian Mathematics.
Calcutta: World Press, 1967.
Steinschneider, M: Jewish Mathematicians.
Enlarged version of some articles in German from 1893-1899.
Memphis, Tennessee: Paideia, 1978.
Suter, H: Die Mathematiker und Astronomen der Araber und ihre Werke.
Abhandlungen zur Geschichte der mathematischen Wissenschaften, Vol. 10.
Leipzig: B.G. Teubner, 1900.
van Der Waerden, B.L: Science Awakening
– Egyptian, Babylonian and Greek Mathematics.
Oxford: Oxford University Press, 1961 (new ed.).
Vogel, Kurt: Vorgriechische Mathematik.
2 vols. Vol.1: Vorgeschichte und Ägypten.
Vol. 2: Die Mathematik der Babylonier.
Hannover: Hermann Schroedel, 1959.

History of Mathematics, Special Topics

Baron, Margaret E: The Origins of the infinitesimal Calculus.
Oxford: Pergamon Press, 1969.
Biggs, Norman L; Lloyd, E. Keith;and Wilson, Robin J: Graph Theory 1736-1936.
Oxford, Clarendon Press, 1976.
Birkhoff, Garrett (ed.): A Source Book in Classical Analysis.
Cambridge, Massachusetts: Harvard University Press, 1973.

Bonola, R.: Non-Euclidean Geometry.
A Critical and Historical Study. Translated
from Italian.
New York: Dover, 1955 (reprint).
Cajori, Florian: A History of Mathematical
Notations.
2 vols. Chicago: Open Court, 1928-30.
Goldstine, Herman H: The Computer from
Pascal to von Neumann.
Princeton: Princeton University Press,
1972.
Goldstine, Herman H: A History of
Numerical Analysis from the 16th through
the 19th Century.
Berlin: Springer, 1977
Hacking, Ian: The Emergence of
Probability. A Philosophical Study of Early
Ideas about Probability, Induction and
Statistical Inference.
London: Cambridge University Press, 1975.
Kendall, M.G. and Pearson, E.S. (eds.):
Studies in the History of Statistics and
Probability.
London: Griffin, 1970.
Kendall, Maurice and Plackett, R.L. (eds.):
Studies in the History of Statistics and
Probability.
Vol. 2. London: Griffin, 1977.
Monna, A.F: Functional Analysis in
Historical Perspective.
Utrecht: Oesthoek, Scheltema and
Holkema, 1973, 1975.
Mostowski, Andrzej: Thirty Years of
Foundational Studies.
Oxford: Blackwell, 1966.
Ore, Oystein: Number Theory and its
History:
New York: Mc Graw-Hill, 1948.
Owen, D.B. (ed.): On the History of
Statistics and Probability.
Proceedings of a symposium. New York:
M.Dekker, 1976.
Surma, Stanislaw J (ed.): Studies in the
History of Mathematical Logic.
Warszawa: Polish Academy of Sciences –
Institute of Philosophy and Sociology,
1973.
Walker, H.M: Studies in the History of
Statistical Method with Special Reference
to Certain Educational Problems.
Baltimore, 1929. New York: Arno Press,
1975 (reprint).
Westergaard, H: Contributions to the
History of Statistics.
London, 1932. Brooklyn Heights, New
York: Beekman Pubs., 1970 (reprint).
Wussing, H.L: Die Genesis des abstrakten
Gruppenbegriffes.
Berlin: VEB Deutscher Verlag der
Wissenschaften, 1969.

Philosophy of Mathematics, in General

Bernays, Paul: Abhandlungen zur
Philosophie der mathematik.
Darmstadt: Wissenschaftliche
Buchgesellschaft, 1976.
Carnap, R: The Foundations of Logic
and Mathematics.
Chicago: International Encyclopedia of
Unified Science 4:3, 1939.
Fang, Joong: Towards a Philosophy of
Modern Mathematics.
Vol.1: Bourbaki. Vol. 2: Hilbert. Memphis,
Tennessee: Paideia, 1970.
Heitsch, W: Mathematik und
Weltanschauung.
Berlin: Akademie-Verlag, 1976.
Hintikka, J (ed.): The Philosophy of
Mathematics.
London: Oxford University Press, 1969.
Lakatos, I (ed.): Problems in the
Philosophy of Mathematics.
Proceedings of a colloquium. Amsterdam:
North-Holland, 1967, 1972.
Lorenzen, P: Metamathematik.
Mannheim: Bibliographisches Institut,
1962.

(Les) Mathématiques et la Réalité. Actes
du Colloque 17-18 mai 1974.
Centre Universitaire de Luxembourg,
162 A, Avenue de la Faiencerie,
Luxembourg, 1974.
Putnam, Hilary: Mathematics, Matter and
Method.
London: Cambridge University Press, 1975.
Russell, B: Introduction to Mathematical
Philosophy.
London: George Allen & Unwin, 1919,
1948.
van Heijenoort, J. (ed.): From Frege to Gö-
del: A Source Book in Mathematical Lo-
gic, 1879-1931.
Cambrigde, Massachusetts: Harvard
University Press, 1967, 1977.
Wang, Hao: From Mathematics to
Philosophy.
London: Routledge & Kegan Paul, 1974.
Weyl, Hermann: Philosophie der
Mathematik und Naturwissenschaft.
Enlarged version of article from 1928.
München: Oldenbourg Verlag,
1976 (4th ed.).
Wittgenstein, L: Bemerkungen über die
Grundlage der Mathematik.
Frankfurt: Suhrkamp Verlag, 1974.

Philosophy of Mathematics, Special Topics

Bishop, Erret: Foundations of Constructive
Analysis.
New York: Mc Graw-Hill, 1967.
Brouwer, L.E.J:: Collected Works. Vol. 1:
Philosophy and Foundations of
Mathematics. Ed: A. Heyting. Vol. 2:
Geometry, Analysis, Topology and
Mechanics. Ed: H. Freudenthal.
Amsterdam: North-Holland, 1975-76.
Carnap, R: Logical Foundations of
Probability.

Chicago 1950. London: Routledge &
Kegan Paul, 1971 (2nd ed.).
Castonguay, C: Meaning and Existence in
Mathematics.
Berlin and Wien: Springer, 1972.
Cohen, Hermann: Das Prinzip der
Infinitesimalmethode und seine
Geschichte.
1883. Frankfurt am Main: Suhrkamp,
1968.
Fang, J: The Illusory Infinite: A Theology
of Mathematics.
Memphis, Tennessee: Paideia, 1976.
Gonseth, Ferd.: Les mathématiques et la
réalité.
Essai sur la méthode axiomatique. Paris:
A. Blanchard, 1977 (new ed).
Hacking, Ian: Logic of Statistical Inference.
London: Cambridge University Press, 1965.
Heyting, A: Intuitionism.
Amsterdam: North-Holland, 1966
(2nd ed.), 1971.
Hilbert, David: Grundlagen der Geometrie.
1899. Leipzig and Berlin: B.G. Teubner,
1968.
Hilbert, D and Bernays, P: Grundlagen der
Mathematik.
2 vols. 1928. Berlin: Springer, 1968-70.
Klaus, G: Kybernetik und
Erkenntnistheorie.
Berlin: VEB Deutscher Verlag der
Wissenschaften, 1972.
Lakatos, I: Proofs and Refutations.
The Logic of Mathematical Discovery.
London: Cambridge University Press, 1976.
Lorenzen, Paul and Schwemmer, Oswald:
Konstruktive Logik, Ethik und
Wissenschaftstheorie.
Mannheim: Bibliographisches Institut,
1973.
Meschkowski, H (ed.): Das Problem des
Unendlichen.
Mathematische Texte von Bolzano, Cantor,
Dedekind.
München: DTV, 1974.
Mises, R. von: Wahrscheinlichkeit, Statistik

und Wahrheit.
1936. Berlin and Wien: Springer, 1972.
Russell, Bertrand: An Essay on the
Foundations of Geometry.
1897. New York: Dover, 1956 (reprint).
Stachowiak, H: Allgemeine Modelltheorie.
Berlin: Springer, 1973.
Stegmüller, W: Unvollständigkeit und
Unentscheidbarkeit.
Die metamathematischen Resultate von
Gödel, Church, Kleene, Rosser und ihre
erkenntnistheoretische Bedeutung.
Berlin: Springer, 1973.
Tarski, Alfred: Introduction to Logic and
to the Methodology of Deductive Sciences.
Oxford: Oxford University Press, 1965.
Thiel, Rainer: Quantität oder Begriff. Der
heuristische Gebrauch mathematischer
Begriffe in Analyse und Prognose
gesellschaftlicher Prozesse.
Berlin: VEB Deutscher Verlag der
Wissenschaften, 1967.
Thiel, R: Mathematik − Sprache −
Dialektik.
Berlin: Akademie Verlag, 1975.
Troelstra, Anne Sjerp: Principles of
Intuitionism.
Berlin: Springer, 1969.

Miscellanies about Mathematics

**Aleksandrov, A.D; Kolmogorov, A.N; and
Lavrentjev, M.A. (eds.)**: Mathematics: Its
Content, Methods and Meaning.
3 vols. Translated from Russian.
Cambridge, Massachusetts: MIT Press,
1969.
Bartlett, M.S.: Essays on Probability and
Statistics.
London: Halsted Press, 1956, 1962.
Carleson, Lennart: Matematik för vår tid.

En presentation och ett debattinlägg.
In Swedish. (Mathematics for Our Time.
A Presentation and a Contribution to
Discussion).
Stockholm: Prisma, 1968.
**Cohen, R.S.; Stachel, J.J; and Wartofsky,
M.W**: For Dirk Struik.
Scientific, Historical and Political
Essays in Honor of Dirk J. Struik.
Dordrecht, Holland: D. Reidel, 1974.
Dieudonné, Jean: Panorama des
mathématiques pures. Le choix
bourbachique.
(Discours de la Methode), Paris:
Gauthier-Villars, 1978.
Hardy, G.H: A Mathematician's Apology.
London: Cambridge University Press,
1940, 1973.
Hogben, L: Mathematics for the Million:
A Popular Self Educator.
London: Allen & Unwin, 1936.
Klein, Felix: Das Erlanger Programm.
Leipzig: Teubner, 1974 (reprint).
Kuntzmann, Jean: Où vont les
mathématiques?
Réflexions sur l'enseignement et la
recherche.
Paris: Hermann, 1967.
Lebesgue, Henri: Message d'un
mathématicien.
(Philosophie, Histoire, Enseignement
Mathématique). Introduction et
extraits choisis par Lucienne Félix.
Paris: A. Blanchard, 1977.
Le Lionnais, Francois (ed.): Les grands
courants de la pensée mathématique.
Paris: A. Blanchard, 1962 (2nd. ed.).
Newman, James R (ed.): The World of
Mathematics.
4 vols. New York, 1956. London:
George Allen & Unwin, 1960.
Otte, Michael (ed.): Mathematiker über
die Mathematik.
Berlin: Springer, 1974.
Steen, L.A. (ed.): Mathematics Today −

Twelve Informal Essays.
Berlin: Springer, 1978.
Weizenbaum, Joseph: Computer Power and
Human Reason.
From Judgment to Calculation.
San Francisco: Freeman, 1976.

Sociology of Mathematics

Fang, J: Sociology of Mathematics and
Mathematicians.
Memphis, Tennessee: Paideia, 1975.

Janco, Manuel and Furjot, Daniel:
Informatique et capitalisme.
Paris: Maspero, 1972.
Moissejew, Nikita Nikolajevic: Mathematik,
Steuerung, Planung, Prognose.
Berlin: Akademie Verlag, 1973.
Politics of Mathematics: A Prolegomenon.
(A revised reprint of Phil.Math. Vol. 15).
Memphis, Tennessee: Paideia, 1979.
Quiniou, J.C: Marxisme et informatique.
Paris: Editions Sociales, 1971.
Samuel, Pierre (ed.): Mathématiques,
mathématiciens et société.
Université Paris XI, UER Mathématique,
Orsay, France, 1974.

Mathematics and Society and Politics

Adams, J. Mack: Social Effects of
Computer Use and Misuse.
New York: Wiley, 1976.
Alker, H.R: Mathematics and Politics.
London: Macmillan, 1965.
Condorcet, M.J.A.N. de Caritat:
Mathématique et société.
Choix de textes et commentaires par R.
Rashed.
Paris: Hermann, 1974.
**Fairley, William B. and Mosteller,
Frederick:** Statistics and Public Policy.
Reading, Massachusetts: Addison-Wesley,
1977.
Høyrup, Else and Jens: Matematikken i
samfundet.
Elementer af en analyse: historie/
undervisning/ideologi. In Danish.
(Mathematics in Society. Elements of an
Analysis: History/Teaching/Ideology).
Copenhagen: Gyldendal, 1973.

Psychology of Mathematics

Auerbach, Felix: Die Furcht vor der
Mathematik und ihre Überwindung.
Jena, 1924. Wiesbaden: Martin Sändig
Reprint, 1967.
Hadamard, Jacques S: An Essay on: The
Psychology of Invention in the
Mathematical Field.
Princeton: Princeton University Press,
1945, 1949. New York: Dover (reprint).
Krutetskii, V.A.: The Psychology of
Mathematical Abilities in Schoolchildren.
Translated from Russian.
Chicago: University of Chicago Press, 1976.
Piaget, Jean: The Child's Conception of
Geometry.
Translated from French.
London: Routledge, 1960.
Piaget, Jean: The Child's Conception of
Number.
Translated from French.
London: Routledge, 1965.

Poincaré, Henri: Mathematical Creation.
An essay first published in "Science et
Méthode".
Paris: Flammarion, 1908. Also published
in Vernon, P.E. (ed.): "Creativity".
Harmondsworth, Middlesex: Penguin, 1970.
Tobias, Sheila: Overcoming Math Anxiety.
New York: Norton, 1978.
van der Waerden, B.L.: Einfall und
Überlegung.
Drei kleine Beiträge zur Psychologie
des mathematischen Denkens.
Basel: Birkhäuser, 1968, 1973.

Mathematics Teaching

Baruch, Stella: Echec et Math.
Paris: Editions du Seuil, 1973.
Chincin, A.Ja: The Teaching of
Mathematics.
Edited by B.V. Gnedenko. Translated from
Russian.
London: The English University Press,
1968.
Cramer, Hans: Zur Mathematisierung des
Mathematikunterrichts.
Versuch einer Didaktik.
Bamberg: Buchner, 1951.
Dienes, Z.P: An Experimental Study of
Mathematics Learning.
London: Hutchinson, 1963, 1968.
Downes, L.W. and Paling, D: The Teaching
of Arithmetic in Tropical Primary Schools.
Oxford: Oxford University Press, 1959.
Fang, J: Numbers Racket.
The Aftermath of "New Math".
Port Washington, New York: Kennikat
Press, 1968.

Freudenthal, H: Mathematics as an
Educational Task.
Dordrecht, Holland: D. Reidel, 1973.
Freudenthal, Hans: Weeding and Sowing.
Preface to a Science of Mathematical
Education.
Dordrecht, Holland: D. Reidel, 1978.
Greenberg, H.J. (preface): Education in
Applied Mathematics.
Proceedings of a conference.
Philadelphia: SIAM = Society for Industrial
and Applied Mathematics, 1967.
Griffith, H.B. and Howson, A.G:
Mathematics, Society and Curricula.
London: Cambridge University Press, 1974.
Howson, A.G. (ed.): Developments in
Mathematical Education.
Proceedings of a congress.
London: Cambridge University Press, 1973.
**IFIP = International Federation for
Information Pocessing:** World Conference
on Computer Education.
Amsterdam, 1970. Amsterdam: IFIP,
1970.
Johnson, D.C. and Tinsley, J.D: Informatics
and Mathematics in Secondary Schools.
Impacts and Relationships. Procedings of
a conference held in Bulgaria.
Amsterdam: North-Holland, 1978.
Kapur, J.N: Thoughts on Mathematical
Education.
Delhi: Atma Ram, 1973.
**Kilpatrick, Jeremy and Wirszup, Izaak
(eds.):** Soviet Studies in the Psychology of
Learning and Teaching Mathematics.
14 vols. Published by School Mathematics
Study Group and Survey of Recent East
European Mathematical Literature.
Chicago: University of Chicago Press, 1969-.
Kline, Morris: Why Johnny Can't Add:
The Failure of the New Math.
New York: St. Martin's Press, 1973.

Kline, Morris: Why the Professor Can't Teach.
Mathematics and the Dilemma of University Education.
New York: St. Martin's Press, 1977.
Lauter, Josef and Röhrl, Emanuel: Kummer mit der neuen Mathematik.
Freiburg: Herder, 1974.
Magne, Olof; Bengtsson, Margot; and Carleke, Ivar: Hur man undervisar elever med matematiksvårigheter.
In Swedish. (How to Teach Pupils with Math Problems).
Stockholm: Esselte, 1973.
McLone, R.R: The training of Mathematicians.
A Research Report.
Social Science Research Council, London, 1973.
NCTM = National Council of Teachers of Mathematics (US): The Slow Learner in Mathematics.
35th Yearbook of NCTM, Reston, Virginia, 1972.
Piaget, J; Beth, E.W; Dieudonné, J; Lichnerowicz, A.; Choquet, G.; and Gattegno, C: L'enseignement des mathématiques.
Lausanne: Delachaux and Niestlé, 1955, 196o.
Polya, George: Mathematical Discovery.
On Understanding, Learning and Teaching Problem Solving. 2 vols.
New York: John Wiley, 1962-65.
Probleme des Mathematikunterrichts.
Diskussionsbeiträge sowjetischer Wissenschaftler.
Translated from Russian.
Berlin: Volk und Wissen, 1965.
Råde, Lennart (ed.): The Teaching of Probability and Statistics.
Proceedings of a conference.
Stockholm and New York: Almqvist & Wiksell and Wiley, 1970.
Schubring, Gert: Das genetische Prinzip in der Mathematik-Didaktik.
Dissertation.
Stuttgart: Klett-Cotta, 1978.
Skemp, Richard R: The Psychology of Learning Mathematics.
Harmondsworth, Middlesex: Penguin, 1971, 1975.
Steiner, Gerhard: Mathematik als Denkerziehung.
Eine psychologische untersuchung uber die Rolle des Denkens in der mathematischen Früherziehung.
Stuttgart: Ernst Klett, 1973.
Steiner, Hans-Georg (ed.): Didaktik der Mathematik.
Darmstadt: Wissenschaftliche Buchgesellschaft, 1978.
Suydam, M.N: Annotated Compilation of Research on Secondary School Mathematics 1930-1970.
2. vols. Washington, D.C: US Office of Education, 1972.

History of Mathematics Teaching

Bidwell, James K. and Clason, Robert G: Readings in the History of Mathematics Education.
Reston, Virginia: NCTM = National Council of Teachers of Mathematics, 1970.
Günther, Siegmund: Geschichte des mathematischen Unterrichts im deutschen Mittelalter bis zum Jahre 1525.
Berlin, 1887. Wiesbaden: Martin Sänding Reprint, 1969.
Inhetveen, Heide: Die Reform des gymnasialen Mathematikunterrichts

zwischen 1890 und 1914.
Eine sozioökonomische Analyse.
Bad Heilbrunn: Julius Klinkhardt, 1976.
Yeldham, Florence A: The Teaching of
Arithmetic through Four Hundred Years
(1535-1935).
London: George G. Harrap, 1936.

Recreational Mathematics

Ball, W.W. Rouse: Mathematical
Recreations and Essays.
London: Macmillan, 1928, 1960.
Dynkin, E.B. and Uspenski, W.A:
Mathematische Unterhaltungen.
3 vols. Translated from Russian.
Berlin: Deutscher Verlag der
Wissenschaften, 1968-76.
Frey, P.W. (ed.): Chess Skill in Man and
Machine.
Berlin: Springer, 1977.
Gardner, Martin: New Mathematical
Diversions from Scientific American.
New York: Simon and Schuster, 1971.
Loyd, Sam: Best Mathematical Puzzles of
Sam Loyd.
Selected and edited by Martin Gardner.
New York: Dover, 1959.
Phillips, Hubert ("Caliban"): My Best
Puzzles in Mathematics.
New York: Dover, 1961.

Untraditional Mathematics Books

Booss, Bernhelm: Topologie und Analysis.

Eine Einführung in die Atiyah-Singer-
Indexformel.
Berlin: Springer Verlag, 1977.
Courant, R. and Robbins, H: What is
Mathematics?
New York: Oxford University Press,
1941, 1958. In German: Was ist
Mathematik? Berlin: Springer, 1973.
Dantzig, Tobias: Number, The Language
of Science.
London: George Allen & Unwin, 1940.
**Duncan, Ronald and Weston-Smith,
Miranda (eds.)**: The Encyclopaedia of
Ignorance.
Vol. 1: Physical Sciences.
Oxford: Pergamon, 1977.
Gelbaum, B. and Olmsted, J:
Counterexamples in Analysis.
New York: McGraw-Hill, 1964.
Gårding, Lars: Encounter with
Mathematics.
Berlin: Springer, 1977.
Hilbert, D. and Cohn-Vossen, S: Geometry
and the Imagination.
New York: Chelsea, 1952.
Klein, Felix: Famous Problems of
Elementary Geometry.
New York: Dover, 1956 (reprint).
Knuth, Donald E: Surreal Numbers.
Reading, Massachusetts: Addison-
Wesley, 1974.
Melzak, Z.A: Companion to Concrete
Mathematics.
2 vols. New York: John Wiley, 1973.
Meschkowski, H: Ungelöste und unlösbare
Probleme der Geometrie.
Mannheim: Bibliographisches Institut,
1975.
Rademacher, H. and Toeplitz, O: Von
Zahlen und Figuren. 1933.
New York and Berlin: Springer, 1968.
Scientific American, Readings from:

Mathematics in the Modern World.
With Introductions by Morris Kline.
San Francisco: Freeman, 1948, 1968.
Scientific American, Readings from:
Computers and Computation.
With Introductions by Robert R. Fenichel
and Joseph Weizenbaum.
San Francisco: Freeman, 1950, 1971.
Steen, Lynn Arthur and Seebach, J.
Arthur: Counterexamples in Topology.
New York, 1970. New York and Berlin:
Springer, 1978.
Weyl, Hermann: Symmetry.
Princeton: Princeton University Press,
1952.

Mathematization

Booss, Bernhelm and Krickeberg, Klaus
(eds.): Mathematisierung der
Einzelwissenschaften.
Basel: Birkhäuser Verlag, 1976.
Frey, G: Die Mathematisierung unserer
Welt.
Stuttgart: Urban Bücher, Kohlhammer
Verlag, 1967.

Mathematical Models

Andrews, J.G. and McLone, R:
Mathematical Modelling.
London: Butterworths, 1976.
Bartlett, M.S: Stochastic Population
Models in Ecology and Epidemiology.
London: Methuen, 1960.

Forrester, Jay W: World Dynamics.
Cambridge, Massachusetts: Wright-
Allen Press, 1971.
Fox, K.A; Sengupta, J.K; and
Narasimham, G.V.L. (eds.): Economic
Models, Estimation and Risk Programming.
Essays in Honor of Gerhard Tintner.
Berlin: Springer, 1969.
Freudenthal, H (ed.): The Concept and the
Role of the Model in Mathematics and
Natural and Social Sciences.
Dordrecht, Holland: Reidel, 1961.
Hawkes, Nigel (ed.): International Seminar
on Trends in Mathematical Modelling.
Berlin: Springer, 1973.
Hyvärinen, L: Mathematical Modeling for
Industrial Processes.
Berlin: Springer, 1970.
Kemeny, J.G. and Snell, J.L: Mathematical
Models in the Social Sciences.
New York, 1962. Cambridge,
Massachusetts: MIT Press, 1972.
Kendall, M.G. et al (eds.): Mathematical
Model Building in Economics and Industry.
2 vols. Proceedings of a conference.
London: Griffin, 1968-70.
Klir, Jiri and Valach, Miroslav: Cybernetic
Modelling.
London/Prague: Illiffe Books/SNTL-
Publishers of Technical Literature, 1967.
Martin, Francis E: Computer Modelling and
Simulation.
New York: Wiley, 1968.
Meadows, Dennis L et al: The Limits to
Growth:
A Report for the Club of Rome's Project
on the Predicament of Mankind.
London: A Potomac Associates Book,
1972.
Roberts, Fred S: Discrete Mathematical
Models.
With Applications to Social, Biological

and Environmental Problems.
Englewood Cliffs, New Jersey: Prentice-
Hall, 1976.
Siegfried, P: Abstraktion, Mathematik,
mathematische Modellierung
gesellschaftlicher Systeme und Prozesse.
Ausgewählte philosophische und
methodologische Probleme.
Dresden, 1972.
Stone, R: Mathematical Models of the
Economy and other Essays.
London: Chapman and Hall, 1970.
Thom, René; Modèles mathématiques de
la morphogenèse.
Recueil de textes sur la théorie des
catastrophes et ses applications.
Paris: Union Générale d'Editions, 1974.
**Tikhonov, A.N; Kuhnert, F; Kuznecov,
N.N; Moszynski, A; and Wakulicz, A.
(eds.)**: Mathematical Models and
Numerical Methods.
Proceedings of a symposium.
Warszawa: PWN- Polish Scientific
Publishers, 1978.

Systems, in General

Ackoff, Russell L. and Emery, Fred E:
On Purposeful Systems.
Chicago: Aldine-Atherton, 1972.
Bensoussan, A. and Lions, J.L. (eds.):
New Trends in Systems Analysis.
Proceedings of a symposium.
Berlin: Springer Verlag, 1977.
Berlinski, David: On Systems Analysis:
An Essay Concerning the Limitations of
some Mathematical Methods in the Social,
Political, and Biological Sciences.

Cambrigde, Massachusetts: MIT Press,
1977.
Bertalanffy, L. von: General System
Theory.
Foundations, Development,
Applications. 1968.
Harmondsworth, Middlesex: Penguin,
1971.
Chorafas, Dimitris N: Systems and
Simulation.
New York: Academic Press, 1965.
Delattre, P: Système, structure,
fonction, évolution.
Recherches interdisciplinaires.
Paris: Maloine-Doin éditeurs, 1971.
Forrester, Jay W: Principles of
Systems.
Cambridge, Massachusetts: Wright Allen
Press, 1968, 1973.
Klir, George J (ed.): Applied General
Systems Research:
Recent Developments and Trends.
New York: Plenum, 1978.
Lange, Oskar Richard: Wholes and Parts.
A General Theory of System Behaviour.
Oxford: Pergamon Press, 1965.
Laszlo, E. (ed.): The Relevance of General
Systems Theory:
Papers Presented to Ludwig von
Bertalanffy on his 70th Birthday.
New York: Braziller, 1972.
Mesarovic, M.D. and Takahara, Yasuhiko:
General Systems Theory:
Mathematical Foundations.
New York: Academic Press, 1975.
Systemtheorie.
Berlin: Colloquium Verlag, Otto H.
Hess, 1972.
Zadeh, L.A. and Polak, E: System Theory.
New York: Mc Graw-Hill, 1969.

Systems, Special Topics

Billeter, Ernst; Cuenod, Michel; and Klaczko, Salomon: Overlapping Tendencies in Operations Research, Systems Theory and Cybernetics.
Proceedings of a symposium.
Basel: Birkhäuser Verlag, 1976.
Bossel, Hartmut; Klaczko, Salomon; and Müller, Norbert (eds.): System Theory in the Social Sciences.
Stochastic Pattern Recognition, Fuzzy Analysis Simulation, Behaviour and Control Systems Models.
Basel: Birkhäuser Verlag, 1976.
Hermann, Robert: Geometry, Physics & Systems.
New York: M. Dekker, 1973.
Kuhn, H.W. and Szegö, G.P. (eds.): Mathematical Systems Theory and Economics.
2 vols. Proceedings of a summer school.
Berlin: Springer, 1969.
Mesarovic, M. et al (eds.): System Theory and Biology.
Berlin: Springer, 1968.
Modern Trends in Cybernetics and Systems.
Proceedings of a congress in Bucharest.
3 vols.
Berlin: Springer, 1977.
Wets, R.J.B. (ed.): Stochastic Systems.
Vol. 1: Modeling, Identification. Vol. 2: Optimization.
Amsterdam: North-Holland, 1976.

Mathematics and Women

AMS = American Mathematical Society:

Directory of Women Mathematicians.
Providence, Rhode Island: American Mathematical Society, 1973-.
Dick, Auguste: Emmy Noether, 1882-1935.
Basel: Birkhäuser Verlag, 1970.
Fox, Lynn H; Fennema, Elizabeth; and Sherman, Julia: Women and Mathematics: Research Perspectives for Change.
The National Institute of Education, US Department of Health, Education, and Welfare; Washington D.C., Nov. 1977.
(NIE Papers in Education and Work, No.8)
Høyrup, Else: Women, Mathematics, Science and Engineering.
A Partially Annotated Bibliography with Emphasis on Mathematics and with References on Related Topics.
Roskilde, Denmark: Roskilde University Library, 1978.
King, A.C; Grinstein, L.S; and Campbell, P.J: Women and Mathematics:
A Critical Inquiry.
Memphis, Tennessee: Paideia, 1978.
Kovalevsky, Sonia: Biography and Autobiography.
2 Parts. Part 1: Memoir, by Anna C. Leffler. Part 2: Reminiscences of Childhood, written by herself.
London: Walter Scott, 1895. The autobiography is translated into German: Erinnerungen an meine Kindheit.
Weimar, 1961.
Osen, Lynn M: Women in Mathematics.
Cambridge, Massachusetts: MIT Press, 1974.
Polubarinova-Kochina, P: Sophia Vasilyevna Kovalevskaya.
Moscow: Foreign Languages Publishing House, 1957.
Somerville, Mary: Personal Recollections from Early Life to Old Age.

London: John Murray, 1874.

COUNTRIES, Past (from 1500) and Present

Africa

Gay, John and Cole, Michael: The New Mathematics and an Old Culture.
A Study of Learning among the Kpelle of Liberia.
New York: Holt, Rinehart & Winston, 1967.
Raum, O.F: Arithmetic in Africa.
London: Evan Bros., 1938.
Zaslavsky, Claudia: Africa Counts.
Number and Pattern in African Culture.
Boston: Prindle, Weber & Schmidt, 1973.

Bulgaria

Iliev, Ljubomir: On the Development of Mathematics in the People's Republic of Bulgaria.
Sofia: Publishing House of the Bulgarian Academy of Sciences, 1975.

Canada

Beltzner, Klaus P; Coleman, A. John; and Edwards, Gordon D: Mathematical Sciences in Canada.
Science Council of Canada, Ottawa, 1976.

China

Fitzgerald, A. and Maclane, S: Pure and Applied Mathematics in the People's

Republic of China.
Washington, D.C.: National Academy of Sciences, 1977.
Swetz, Frank: Mathematics Education in China: Its Growth and Development.
Cambridge, Massachusetts: MIT Press, 1974.
Tsao, C.K: Contemporary Chinese Research Mathematics.
Vol. 1: Bibliography of Mathematics Published in Communist China During the Period 1949-1960. Providence, Rhode Island: American Mathematical Society, 1961.

England

Taylor, E.G.R: The Mathematical Practitioners of Tudor & Stuart England.
London: Cambridge University Press, 1954.
Taylor, E.G.R: The Mathematical Practitioners of Hanoverian England 1714-1840.
London: Cambridge University Press, 1966.

France

Nielsen, N: Geomètres francais sous la révolution.
Translated from Danish.
Copenhagen: Levin & Munksgaard, 1929.

FRG

Behnke, Heinrich and Steiner, Hans-Georg (eds.): Mathematischer Unterricht an deutschen Universitäten und Schulen.
Göttingen: Vandenhoeck & Ruprecht, 1967.

GDR

Sachs, Horst (ed.): Entwicklung der Mathematik in der DDR.
Berlin: VEB Deutscher Verlag der Wissenschaften, 1974.

Germany

Biermann, K.R: Die Mathematik und ihre Dozenten an der Berliner Universität 1810-1920.
Berlin: Akademie Verlag, 1973.

Italy

Libri, Guglielmo: Histoire des sciences mathématiques en Italie.
Depuis la renaissance des lettres jusqu'à la fin du dix-septième siècle.
Paris, 1838-1841.
New York: Johnson Reprint, 1966.
Rose, Paul Lawrence: The Italian Renaissance of Mathematics. Studies on Humanists and Mathematicians from Petrarch to Galileo.
Genève: Librarie Droz, 1975.

Soviet Union

See the journal Russian Mathematical Surveys,
London.

USA

Cajori, Florian: The Teaching and History of Mathematics in the United States.
Washington: Government Printing Office, 1890. Reprint 1974.
May, Kenneth O (ed.): The Mathematical Association of America — Its First Fifty Years.
Washington, D.C: MAA = Mathematical Association of America, 1972.
NCTM = National Council of Teachers of Mathematics (US): A History of Mathematical Education in the USA and Canada.
NCTM, Reston, Virginia, 1970.
Tarwater, Dalton (ed.): The Bicentennial Tribute to American Mathematics.
Washington, D.C: MAA = Mathematical

Association of America, 1978.

How to Write Mathematics

Dieudonné, J.A; Halmos, P.R; Schiffer, M.M; and Steenrod, N.E: How to Write Mathematics.
Providence, Rhode Island: American Mathematical Society, 1973, 1975.

Bibliographies

Dick, Elie M: Current Information Sources in Mathematics. An Annotated Guide to Books and Periodicals, 1960-1972.
Littleton, Colorado: Libraries Unlimited Inc., 1973.
Dorling, A.R. (ed.): Use of Mathematical Literature.
London: Butterworths, 1977.
Gaffney, M.P. and Steen, L.A: Annotated Bibliography of Expository Writing in the Mathematical Sciences.
Washington, D.C: The Mathematical Association of America, 1976.
May, Kenneth O: Bibliography and Research Manual of the History of Mathematics.
Toronto: University of Toronto Press, 1973.
Schaaf, William L: Bibliography of Recreational Mathematics.
3 vols. Reston, Virginia: NCTM = National Council of Teachers of Mathematics (US), 1970-73.

Dictionaries

Clason, W.E: Elsevier's Dictionary of
Computers, Automatic Control and Data
Processing. In Six Languages.
Amsterdam: Elsevier, 1971, 1973.
James, G. and James, R.C., compiled by:
Mathematics Dictionary.
New York: Van Nostrand, 1968, 1976
(4th ed.).
Kendall, M.G. and Buckland, W.R. (eds.):
A Dictionary of Statistical Terms. 1957.
Harlow, Essex: Longman, 1971 (3rd ed.).
Klaus, Georg and Liebscher, Heinz:
Wörterbuch der Kybernetik. 1967.
Berlin: Dietz Verlag, 1976.
Meschkowski, Herbert:
Mehrsprachenwörterbuch mathematischer
Begriffe.
Mannheim: Bibliographisches Institut,
1972.
**Naas, Joseph and Schmid, Hermann
Ludwig (eds.):** Mathematisches
Wörterbuch. Mit Einbeziehung der
theoretischen Physik. 2 vols.
Berlin: Akademie-Verlag, 1961, 1974.

Handbooks

Barwise, J (ed.): Handbook of
Mathematical Logic.
Amsterdam: North Holland, 1977.
Bronstein, I.N. and Semendjajew, K.A:
Taschenbuch der Mathematik.
Translated from the Russian edition of
1956.
Frankfurt: Harri Deutsch, 1971, 1975.
**Burington, Richard S. and May, Donald
C. (Jr.):** Handbook of Probability and
Statistics with Tables.
New York: Mc Graw-Hill, 1969, 1970.
Dreszer, Jerzy: Mathematik-Handbuch

(für Technik und Naturwissenschaft).
Frankfurt: Harri Deutsch, 1975.
(für Technik und Naturwissenschaft).
Frankfurt: Harri Deutsch, 1975.
Eiselt, H.A. and von Frajer, H: Operations
Research Handbook.
Standard Algorithms and Methods.
Berlin: W. de Gruyter-Verlag, 1977.

Encyclopedias

Gellert, W. et al (eds.): Kleine
Enzyklopädie-Mathematik. 1965.
Leipzig: VEB Bibliographisches Institut,
1977. Translated into English: The VNR
Concise Encyclopedia of Mathematics.
New York: Van Nostrand Reinhold, 1977.
**Iyanaga, Shokichi and Kawada,
Yukiyosi (eds.):** Encyclopaedic Dictionary
of Mathematics. Issued by the
Mathematical Society of Japan. Translated
from Japanese.
Cambridge, Massachusetts: MIT Press,
1977.
Ralston, Anthony (ed.): Encyclopedia of
Computer Science.
New York: Van Nostrand Reinhold, 1977.

Addresses

**The International Mathematical Union
(ed.):** World Directory of Mathematicians.
1966.
Mathematics Department, Kyoto
University, Kyoto, Japan, 1979 (6th ed.).

Appendix 2. List of participants

Ubiratan D'Ambrosio, Brazil. Director of the Mathematics Institute and Computing Center of the State University of Campinas, Vice-President for the "Comité Interamericano de Educación Mathematica". *Calculus of variations.*

Leif Arkeryd, Sweden. Göteborg University, Department of Mathematics. *Dynamical Systems.*

Avi C. Bajpai, England. Director of Camet, University of Technology, Loughborough, Editor of the Int. J. Math.Educ. Sci.Technol. *Mathematics education.*

Werner Böge, FRG. Department of Applied Mathematics at Heidelberg University. *Foundations of probability, systematization of "applied mathematics".*

Bogdan Bojarski, Poland. Head of the Mathematics Institute of Warsaw University. *Partial differential equations.*

Lothar Budach, GDR. Chairman of the Math. Class of the Acad. of Sc. of the GDR, Head of the Algebra Research Group at the Humboldt University at Berlin. *Categories, algebraic geometry, finite automata, complexity.*

Jelto Buurman, FRG. Oldenburg University, President of the Student Council of the Department of Mathematics.

John L. Casti, USA. Dept. of Computer Applications & Information Systems and Department of Quantitative Analysis of New York University. *Applied systems research.* x)

Bent Christiansen, Denmark Royal Danish School of Educational Studies, Vice-President of the International Commission on Mathematical Instruction (ICMI). *Mathematics education.*

Pierre Crépel, France. UER de Mathématique et Informatique, Université de Rennes. *Measure theory, stochastic processes.*

George F.D. Duff, Canada. Department of Mathematics, University of Toronto, Former President of the Canadian Mathematical Congress, FRSC. *Partial differential equations, mathematical problems of tidal energy.*

Judy Green, USA. Rutgers University, Department of Mathematics. Vice-President of the Association for Women in Mathematics. *Logic.*

Paul Green, USA. University of Maryland, Department of Mathematics. *Analysis.*

Else Høyrup, Denmark. Roskilde University Centre, Library. *Information retrieval, sociology of mathematics, sociology of women mathematicians.*

Jens Høyrup, Denmark. Roskilde University Centre, Institute for the History and Philosophy of Sciences. *History of mathematics.*

Herman J.A. Duparc, Netherlands. Mathematics Department of the Delft Institute for Technology. *Information processing.*

Boris V. Gnedenko, USSR. Lomonosov University of Moscow, Member of the Ukrainian Academy of Science. *Probability theory.*

Wolfgang Haken, USA. University of Illinois, Department of Mathematics. *Discrete mathematics.*

A. Geoffrey Howson, England. University of Southampton, Faculty of Mathematical Studies. *Mathematics education.*

Arne Jensen, Denmark. Director of the Department for Mathematical Statistics and Operations Research, Danish Institute for Technology, Copenhagen. *Operations research.*

Maurice Kendall, England. London University College and the International Statistical Institute, Project Director of the World Fertility Survey. *Mathematical statistics and data analysis.*

Philip G. Kirmser, USA. Professor of Engineering and Mathematics, Kansas State University. *Numerical analysis.*

Salomon Klaczko, FRG. Institute for Systems Technique and Innovation Research of the Fraunhofer Society for Applied Research, Karlsruhe. Editor of the Series "Interdisciplinary Systems Research", Birkhäuser Verlag, Basel. *Artificial intelligence, multivariate data analysis, dynamical computer models.*

Ulrich Knauer, FRG. Head of the Department for Mathematics of Oldenburg University. *General Algebra.*

Mogens Esrom Larsen, Denmark. Mathematics Institute of Copenhagen University, Vice-President of the Danish Mathematical Society. *Complex analysis.*

Lee Lorch, Canada. York University and Former Member-at-large of the Council of the American Mathematical Society, FRSC, Former Member of the Council of the Canadian Mathematical Society. *Analysis.*

Rangaswami Narasimhan, India. Bombay, Tata Institute of Fundamental Research, Director of the National Centre for Software Development and Computing Techniques, Chairman of the Admissions Committee and Trustee of the International Federation for Information Processing (IFIP). *Computational modelling of complex behaviour.*[x)]

Frithiof Niordson, Denmark. Head of the Institute for Solid Mechanics of the Danish Center for Applied Mathematics. *Mathematical applications in engineering.*

Tim Poston, England and Switzerland. Battelle Geneva Research Center. *Catastrophe theory.*

G.S. Ramaswamy, India & West Indies. Caribbean Industrial Research Institute, Trinidad, United Nations Development Programme Chief Technical Adviser. *Analysis and design of shell structures and structural optimization.* x)

Leopold Schmetterer, Austria. Head of the Department for Applied Mathematics of Vienna University and Secretary General of the Austrian Academy of Sciences. *Probability theory.*

Ronald A. Scriven, England. Central Electricity Research Laboratories, Leatherhead, Surrey, Vice-President of the Institute of Mathematics and its Applications (Essex).

Reinhard Selten, FRG. Head of the Institute for Mathematical Economics, Bielefeld University. *Game theory, experimental research on economic behaviour.*

Mohammad El Tom, Sudan. Khartoum University, Mathematics Department, Faculty of Engineering, Chairman of the Organizing Committee of the "International Conference on Developing Mathematics in Third World Countries". *Numerical analysis.*

Flemming Topsøe, Denmark. Mathematics Institute of Copenhagen University, President of the Danish Mathematical Society. *Measure theory, information theory.*

Organizing Committee:

Bernhelm Booss, FRG & Denmark. Executive Director of the Interdisciplinary

Mathematization Centre of Bielefeld University and Visiting Professor at Roskilde University Centre. *Global analysis.*

Mogens Niss, Denmark. Institute of Studies in Mathematics and Physics and their Functions in Education, Research and Applications, Roskilde University Centre. *Mathematics education.*

Organizational Board:

Inger Grethe Christensen, RUC. *Secretary.*
Mogens Brun Heefelt, RUC. *Mathematics.*
Jørgen Larsen, RUC. *Mathematical statistics.*
Anders Madsen, RUC. *Mathematics.*
Anne Sidenius, RUC. *Secretary.*

x) Have contributed with working papers but were at the last moment unable to attend.